With vulnerability and insight, Sara Hagerty shares her story and invites the deep parts of us to find the deep parts of Him, where life is found. It is a profound testimony to the love and goodness of an intimate and beautiful God.

—Stasi Eldredge
coauthor, *New York Times* bestseller *Captivating*

Sara poetically takes us on a fresh yet familiar journey—delays, pain, stress, loss—that leads us to the feet of the one whom our soul loves. This book is a tender cry for all of us to find His beauty in the middle of all of our frustrations, and a beautiful reminder that He sees us through it all. You will be deeply encouraged and moved by this stunning book.

—Jennie Allen
author, *Anything* and *Restless*

Each year I choose a "best book of the year" to recommend or give to friends. This year my choice is clear, for *Every Bitter Thing Is Sweet* is a life changer! Sara Hagerty has a depth in her soul, the tongue of a skillful writer, and an amazingly compelling story. Thank you, Sara, for giving us what we need the most, whether we realize it or not: more intimacy with this mysterious God who sees us, shapes us, and shows up in our lives with "bursts of glory."

—Dee Brestin
author, *Idol Lies*, *The God of All Comfort*,
and *The Friendships of Women*

If you have struggled with the goodness of God in the valleys of life, then this book is for you. Sarah beautifully paints how God gently and tenderly revealed Himself in the midst of her seasons of longing and waiting.

—**Noelle Dienert Davis**
granddaughter of Ruth and Billy Graham

From page one, Sara's poetic and vulnerable writing invites readers to truly experience the pain and redemption she has experienced and that we all can relate to. Her hunger to experience God's presence and her description of what that looks like will inspire you to find God in every circumstance of your life, bitter and sweet, and lead others to do the same.

—**Sara Hall**
professional track athlete

Sara Hagerty has traveled an unlikely route to joy. Instead of harboring bitterness and resentment because of her barrenness, Sara learned that out of something painful, something beautiful can grow. The book is like a garden of beauty with so many blossoms of hope that were "birthed" in her barrenness. What God taught Sara in her struggles will inspire any woman with a pulse.

—**Jackie Kendall**
bestselling author, *Lady in Waiting*

God is still in the business of giving beauty for ashes. Sara's story proves it. Stunningly honest and moving. You don't just read this book; you experience it.

—**Stacey Thacker**
coauthor, *Hope for the Weary Mom*

With penetrating vulnerability and insight, Sara Hagerty brings us into the deep wrestling of our hearts in pain and delay, offering us the lifeline she found in the darkness: fellowship with the heart of Jesus. The gold of this book will leave you thirsting for more of God and equipped to find Him even in the hardest times.

—Dana Candler
author, *Deep unto Deep*

This book is an exquisite love story between a woman and her God. Prepare to be swept away by Sara's storytelling and by the God who loves her and you! This is one of my all-time favorite reads by one of my all-time favorite authors.

—Joy Forney
joyforney.org

In her book, Sara poetically draws us into her story of loss, grief, and redemption, and of how God's name was written over every word of it, drawing her to Himself and showing her that He is not only a good God but a God who is good to her.

—Kelly Raudenbush
The Sparrow Fund

Sara Hagerty's journey from barrenness to abundance takes readers through droughts and valleys only to surprise us with streams of living water. Hers is a story of miraculous, persistent grace that makes me want to know God more deeply, especially through the hardest times.

—Amy Julia Becker
author, *Small Talk* and *A Good and Perfect Gift*

In prose as lyrical as it is luminous, Sara Hagerty takes us on an unforgettable — and remarkably personal — journey into the gracious heart of Providence by exposing her struggles with marriage, infertility, and international adoption. At once passionate and intimate, this book is a trail guide to the mysterious wilderness of faith and a confirmation of the treasures that await those who persist in walking the narrow road.

— **Corban Addison**
internationally bestselling author,
Garden of Burning Sand

Sara Hagerty is my favorite new writer. This book is a gripping read that tugged on my heartstrings and helped shift my paradigm about how life's bitter things, over time, can become sweet. I will read everything she writes.

— **Esther Fleece**
CEO of L&L Consulting, Communicator
and Catalyst Backstage Host

EVERY
BITTER
THING
is SWEET

SARA HAGERTY

EVERY
BITTER
THING
is SWEET

TASTING THE GOODNESS OF GOD
IN ALL THINGS

ZONDERVAN

Every Bitter Thing Is Sweet
Copyright © 2014 by Sara Hagerty

ISBN 978-0-310-33995-3 (ebook)

Requests for information should be addressed to:
Zondervan, *3900 Sparks Dr. SE, Grand Rapids, Michigan 49546*

Library of Congress Cataloging-in-Publication Data

Hagerty, Sara, 1977-
 Every bitter thing is sweet : tasting the goodness of God in the midst
of life's losses / Sara Hagerty.—1 [edition].
  pages cm
 Includes bibliographical references and index.
 ISBN 978-0-310-33994-6 (hardcover : alk. paper)
 1. Spirituality—Christianity. 2. Spiritual life—Christianity.
3. Expectation (Psychology)—Religious aspects—Christianity.
4. Loss (Psychology)—Religious aspects—Christianity. 5. Christian
women—Religious life. I. Title.
BV4501.3.H34545 2014
248.4—dc23   2014010468

Published in association with Yates & Yates, www.yates2.com.

Cover design: James Hall
Cover photography: James Hall / Shutterstock®
Interior design: Sarah Johnson

First printing August 2014 / Printed in the United States of America

To Nate:

You unlock me.
You've represented Him so well to my heart.

CONTENTS

FOREWORD

I open my computer on an impossible day, and without fail there is an email from Sara. *How did she know?* I wonder. But really it is not surprising. Sara hears from God. Her spirit is so tuned in to His heart that I am never surprised when the prayers she prays over me via email match up exactly with what I am feeling and thinking and learning, even without my having breathed a word of it to her.

Isn't it amazing how God loves us? It is rare that such a cherished friendship could be forged across an ocean after only very brief interactions. I am amazed that God cares about me so much that He would take the intimate, sacred pleas and whispers of my heart and impart them to someone so far away. And I am amazed at Sara's continued faithfulness to pray for and over me, my heart, and my family. God uses this woman to speak to me, and it is my prayer that as you read her words, her heart laid bare here on these pages, He will speak to you too.

Sara understands deeply something that I am still slowly learning, reaching to grasp. She knows what it is to hope when it doesn't make sense, to seek God with our hearts when our flesh wants to run. She knows what it is to seek Him out of obedience, to trust Him and even hope in Him as a sacrifice of praise. Sara knows who God is in the long dark nights, and that He is that same God on the warm spring mornings that burst with new life.

Sara knows communion with the Father. She calls it adoration, and I know that it moves His heart. Sara has learned that God is much more concerned with who we are becoming than with what we are doing, and she shares it all here as she cries over carrot peelings and rejoices in the miracle of a tiny bit of growth in her child's heart.

I have been learning this lesson for years and I learn it anew in these pages: Our God, he can make baskets of bread out of the tiny loaves we hand Him. He can make a life of glory out of our weak-kneed, timid yes to Him. As C. S. Lewis said, "To love is to be vulnerable" — open to love and then, too, open to disappointment. Too often we try to avoid that scary place where we love so deep, so much, our hearts could break. But without the bitterness, we would never appreciate the sweetness.

It is my great privilege to introduce you to my friend Sara. This is a book for those hearts who long to see Him in the mess. It is Sara's personal story, written with eloquence and grace, about a God who rescued her from barrenness and carried her to a land of abundance, dripping with milk and honey and all things His goodness. She teaches me again what I have already known; she teaches me to hope anew. He is the candle in the darkness, the light that radiates glory and sprinkles new mercies every morning. My prayer is that as you read these words, you will be drawn to a hope, to the Father, whose extravagant love never ceases to amaze.

—Katie Davis

A satisfied soul loathes the honeycomb,
But to a hungry soul every bitter thing is sweet.

—Proverbs 27:7

one

THE QUESTION UNEARTHED

"Blessed are those who hunger."

My life wears stretch marks from a child. A child I never conceived yet spent a decade birthing. A child who, in the swirl of my wounds, has healing for me still.

I don't search for a remedy to remove these marks. Though ugly to some, they are a sign of life.

God scarred me with beauty.

He gave me a story to tell. He wrote on my life.

I am branded.

I stepped through the doorway into her home, tentatively.

While I would classify myself as an introvert, social settings are rarely, if ever, intimidating to me. I love stories. And people always carry stories.

That day as I entered the foyer, I met three women: A distracted twentysomething who was constantly reapplying her lip gloss. A girl, underdressed for the occasion, but fashionably confident in her thrift jeans. A jumpered mother whose sleeve wore the remnant of a child's morning oatmeal and whose gray hairs revealed layers of beauty. Each of them had a story.

At another time, that foyer would have been my social

playground. God-prints were all over these women, who, at this intersection, might move from acquaintances to friends.

But this day was different.

The woman reapplying her lip gloss was pregnant. Her story stopped there for me. The jumper-clad, oatmeal-smudged mom clearly had something I didn't. And the girl, I quickly learned, though youthful in demeanor, had three children at home and had just discovered—to her surprise—her womb had been opened again.

I came dressed with confidence and holding a gift wrapped with class, but alongside these women I felt insecure and empty. I had nothing to offer this crew.

Minutes before, driving through those rolling Shenandoah hills, I wanted to turn around and go home. But I had sent my reply. And my desire to please my expecting friend, who was the guest of honor, and her friend, who was hosting this event, trumped my fantasies of changing out of my church clothes into sweats and gulping down a chai.

Baby showers had become a "no go" for me since my little stint of not being able to conceive grew into a state of being. I almost always had an easy out, with a fully scheduled life, but a few times I had to offer my real explanation for not attending. And then, of course, there were always the necessary exceptions.

This shower was my exception. It was for a dear friend, a small shower, and I knew my absence would be obvious. When I had sent my reply, my heart was in a good place. I felt settled with the lot God had given me, and was even more determinedly pleading in prayer with the belief that my day would come.

But grief's tide can't be predicted. Two weeks later, I wasn't so ready to participate in this baby brigade.

But I was there, smiling. Congratulating.

Then, among the wrapping paper rips, the sips of punch, and the clanking of forks on chocolate-smeared plates, the stories began.

At first they were humorous, ones I could easily laugh alongside. Funny, cute, first-days-of-life-in-the-great-wide-open accounts.

But as the gift-opening slowed, it was only natural that the advice for this new mom-to-be filled the empty space.

There were only eight of us. All of whose wombs had been opened but mine—an observation, it seemed, no one else made. On the one hand, I was glad: *Oh, please, let no one feel sorry for me*, I thought when the conversation shifted, even as the membrane between mind and heart disintegrated and I became deeply sorry for myself. On the other hand, I was searching for a way—any way—to put an end to this conversation.

Please stop.

Someone stop these tales of labor and delivery that single me out. Your rite of passage, for me, holds a sign at the front that says Do Not Enter. It carries with it so many questions, so many doubts, fears, and insecurities. About me, and about God. When I open that door, when I go to that place, alone, I am lost.

As the laughter of shared experience increased, this sorority of sisters formed bonds around their anecdotes. And I drifted inward and downward.

Comparison plagued my soul.

At the first opportunity to graciously excuse myself, I left. Since the women didn't seem to notice my silence, I was certain no one would notice my absence.

Like most pain, until you have known it for yourself, you are blind to it.

In the car, my eyes released tears and my heart soured toward the women I had shared cake with that afternoon. Their stories were no longer alluring to me, and the only God-prints I saw were the ones I lacked.

They were fruitful; I was barren.

In times like this of losing myself in comparison, I didn't see God as a belligerent Father refusing the simple, natural requests of His daughter. He wasn't stern and angry with me, leading out with punishment. He wasn't even absent, His mind caught up in more important matters.

This wasn't about false perceptions of God at all — or so I thought.

It was about me.

My question was not, Is God good? But instead, Is He good to me? I was overlooked. Forgotten. Not important enough to bless, and easy enough to dismiss.

Cursed.

If the mother whose womb had been opened was living her reward, what had the barren one done to carry such a vacancy?

This question wove itself into the backdrop of my every interaction with those who had what I didn't. And it was the question (and its hidden assumptions) I was learning had to be brought into my conversation with God if I would ever find life through barrenness.

The morning after the shower, I returned to a habit that began years earlier when the darkness on the outside forced a reckoning with God on the inside. I padded around the first floor of our house on the hill, in the room-to-room circle my feet now knew from memory. The world was silent, the lingering night sky keeping it placid, while I talked to Him.

This season was still barren on the outside; I could hardly point to one area of my life that was working as it should. But I was full on the inside, finding a rhythm of using the pain of my outside circumstances — such as the sting from the shower — to drive me deeper into this secret conversation with God. Just as each foot found its way into an imaginary groove in the floor as I made that circular loop, I was learning where to take my ache. I was creating a space here, inside, for a new home with Him. After years of having a stone-cold heart toward God's whisper and His Word, I began to feel a shift. I had little left but that Word and that whisper. He had whittled me down.

The Bible resting on my chair showed wear — how could it not? My friend, my best friend in this hour, was the Author. The book I'd once used to plan youth ministry talks, the book I'd once used to quote pithy sayings and to confirm opinions I'd already formed, that book had found its way into my deep.

The God behind it was proving Himself to be fundamentally different than what I'd supposed for at least a decade, maybe more. But I was finding Him. In the places I had feared most and spent a lifetime avoiding, He was meeting me. My worst, my very worst, moments were getting rewritten without circumstances changing. I was getting acquainted with the kind of deep satisfaction that bad news can't shake. He was showing me Himself as strong enough. He was letting me hide in Him, letting me find a safe place.

And so I cradled my midnight questions while mamas cradled their babies, and I let God's psalms tell me He cradled the answer in Himself. I felt forgotten, but I heard God speak that He had not left me. I felt weak, but I heard Him promise an overshadowing. I felt anxious that my constant fumblings would annoy Him, but I heard Him say He delighted in me.

And I felt hungry.

I wasn't this hungry when God was a distant coach, forcing me to perform.

I wasn't this hungry when I had a life easily explained, easily predicted.

I wasn't this hungry when everyone understood me.

Pain had created space. Space to want more. Space to taste a sense of being *alive*. An alive that would grow to be my favorite kind of alive: secret, hidden to all eyes but mine and those nearest to me.

This had to be the hope of a lifetime, Him and Him alone.

But redemption is full of dimensions.

Little did I know that staring at Him, looking deeply, wouldn't always be a secret. This new perspective was infectious, inside and out.

Little did I know that I was to see the goodness of the Lord in the land of the living.

A brown hand reached around the gate to pull it open at the sound of our driver's horn. I moved from a posture of absorbing all that was around me—this slice of Africa I'd just met hours earlier—to homing in on the purpose of our travel excursion. My little girl's bed was in this house, enclosed. My son's playing field was in front of me.

We were led by the house mother through the hallway to their rooms. All these months of waiting had allowed me to fashion this moment one hundred different ways in my mind, none of which I was experiencing now. I had pictured a waiting room, a place where we would collect ourselves before stepping across the threshold of an introduction that would change our lives forever.

As I peeked in and out of rooms, wondering where we'd perch and wait, a split-second interaction would leave me with an armful.

"Meske!?" the house mother shouted from across the hall while stepping into one of the rooms and scooping up all seventeen pounds of Eden's three-year-old body. She thrust her into my arms.

We'd planned that I'd first hold our new son, Caleb, and that Nate would first hold Eden, our new daughter. So I nervously handed Eden what was intended to be Caleb's gift, a bear. My peace offering wasn't necessary. It was me that she wanted.

She wrapped fingers, too small for her age, around the upper part of my arm and didn't let go. (And she wouldn't. For hours.)

My little girl glowed. Her eyes held an expectant look that said, "Can we make up for my lifetime in this one afternoon?" The rise and fall of her chest against me overshadowed the fact that she didn't speak. She breathed safely. She rested. Everything about her little person said amen.

And he? Caleb was Daddy's boy from the minute he saw his white-skinned counterpart. I noted something in him, then, which has taken years of understanding his story for me to name. Caleb met fatherly love for the first time when he met Nate, the kind of love in which you could wrap yourself and find healing by its very nearness.

Nate overshadowed Caleb's story that day. A new day had come. We didn't know how new it was for him until years later. Like any good story, time revealed its layers.

I'm not sure how long we stayed in that home, but things like naptime, potty, and snacks weren't yet on my priority list. We didn't let go of our son and daughter even as we also cuddled the other children who wandered in and out of the room. We wanted our two to know that we were different from the others who'd passed through. As they climbed over and around our laps, we frequently interrupted them to whisper in their ears in broken Amharic: "I am your mommy." "I am your daddy."

What we said, they already seemed to know. As if they were newborns who had spent months incubating inside of their mother, our scent—to them—was like their own. The umbilical cord stretched over a wide ocean but was there, nonetheless. The Father had forged a connection, even before our eyes stared into theirs.

After we bridged what felt like years in just a few hours of nearness, we said our goodbyes to the nannies who had loved them so well. I wondered whether Caleb and Eden knew those goodbyes were forever.

Then we went to the guest home where we were staying and gave the children baths. We dressed them in the pajamas that had been folded in a stack at our home for them for months, in the room that had been our guest room for years. The room that now had plaques with their names painted on them, hung on the wall.

He slept heavily. She spent her first night fighting sleep so she could peer out from the covers every hour or so to make sure we were still there. I'll never forget the sound of the sheets around her little body as she jolted up in bed, paused to get her bearings, and searched out our silhouettes under the sheets in the bed across from her.

We had become a family, in a moment, yet I still didn't know Caleb's birthmarks or Eden's freckles. I couldn't serve them their favorite meal or find their ticklish spots. They hadn't yet heard my deep belly laugh or become familiar with the way Nate glanced at me, sideways, when he was trying to read my response to something he'd said.

We were also getting acquainted with us as *four.* Each of us was a new part of a new whole, though God had known us as "us" since the beginning of time. We had a history together, though we'd lived apart. We'd each known brokenness and loss, yet with no concept of how those paths would merge into each other's beauty one day.

Healing that had been coursing inside of me, spanning years, surfaced that July in Ethiopia. When my lips brushed Eden's forehead for the first time, a holy vindication echoed through-out the heavens. My life surfaced a win, His win. It had always been there, but now I could touch it. Evidence that God not only loved me but liked me and enjoyed me—something I'd spent decades subtly refuting—now worked its way into my visible story. I got to sweep aside the ashes of years and try on beauty.

And it fit. Just right.

I had grown to know God when no one was looking and when life still wasn't "working" as I'd suspected it should. There, He was the God who saw me and *knew* me and reveled in what He knew. That understanding, as it worked its way into my insides, though not my circumstances, steadied me.

And now, here I was, in the unfolding fulfillment of many (though not all) circumstances, living wildly alive. God's signature over my barrenness, over my broken story, once unknown, was now a spiritual branding on my flesh.

It said: God is good ... to me.

For Your Continued Pursuit

Isaiah 61:3 | Romans 9:20–21 | Psalm 32:7 | Job 23:12 | Psalm 27:13 | Psalm 91:2 | Hebrews 6:19 | Genesis 8:11 | Zephaniah 3:17 | 2 Corinthians 4:17 | 2 Corinthians 2:15 | Colossians 1:16 | Jeremiah 29:11

This section at the end of each chapter is for those readers who, like me, want to trace any spoken declarations back to God's truth and use those as starting points for adoring Him, for making His Word part of their everyday language. Some verses are quoted within each chapter, and others are implied.

two

MOMENTS OF YES

"Draw me away!"

The November when I was fifteen, I stood underneath the canopied expanse of Michigan sky, and the very big God who created it came near.

Hundreds of us, teenagers, had just filed outside from a sweaty dining hall where one not too much older than us casually stood up front with his Bible and told us about this Jesus who didn't just come to imprint history but came to enter our hearts. We were there for a weekend of fun with our friends, just a retreat. Many of us were unsuspecting. We didn't know that this weekend might forever change us.

As tears dropped one by one off my cheek and onto my woolen mittens, I heard the movements of those around me who were also considering this message. The shifting of boots in the snow mingled with sniffles and stifled sobs. The dark sky created a hiding place for the hundreds of hearts in that field who for the first time this night had their eyes opened to God, whose eyes had been fixed on them since before they were born. The curtain was pulled back and a new dawn offered, in the night.

I'd grown up in church. I believed in Jesus. I had my own Bible. I paid homage to His death year after year before devouring scores of peanut-butter-filled chocolate eggs. Our big events revolved around His big events. God was commonplace in our home.

But God's appeal for relationship, however many times I had heard it before, was new that night.

As I stood in my fifteen-year-old frame, which was wrapped in layers of long johns, and considered Him, His unraveling of me began.

I could not name it at the time, as I walked back to the gathering place alone, alongside the others, but this was just the beginning of a life of regeneration.

I knew then that I wanted something new. I know now that we were made for newness.

The next day, I wrote carefully in red ink on the front of a yellow legal pad that became my first journal: "November 13, 1992. My new relationship with Jesus Christ."

It may have been more appropriate to write: "November 13, 1992. The beginning of a lifetime of 'new.'"

My young heart didn't receive then that, yes, the new would come, but both death and life would run as commingling streams throughout the decades ahead. For the new to come, the old in me had to go. I would be left with an uncomfortable hunger, a longing, for new life yet to be born.

The summer after I etched that date on the yellow legal pad, it was all still fresh. The Bible I'd gotten for my confirmation years earlier now showed signs of wear. I held it, casually and comfortably, just as I'd seen the man do that November night when he spoke to the room of sweaty high school bodies that were steaming up the windows of Camp Storer. My Bible *was*

becoming comfortable for me to hold. His Word had begun to be familiar. I enjoyed it.

I'd always been a reader, but this was different. I mimicked what I'd seen friends—some who were also new to the practice of inviting God into their adolescent, everyday world—do with their Bibles. I highlighted verses and put stars next to phrases that spoke to me. I switched from the legal pad to a journal, where I wrote prayers to Him, like letters. His Word was easing its way into my normal high school experience. The idea of a relationship with this God was becoming normal to me, though still mysterious.

As the summer musk grew from June into July that year, I found myself often escaping to our backyard swing after I'd gone out for the night with friends. The spotlight from the porch just below my parents' window, combined with the moonlight, illuminated the Bible cracked open in my lap.

I didn't wear my watch.

This wasn't a duty; I just wanted more of this Jesus who filled the pages. I stayed up late into the night reading and talking with Him and journaling. I couldn't get enough.

I'd defined summers prior to this one by a certain boy I liked or a vacation my family took. This summer was different. I was falling in love. But this time with God.

I didn't have rules or parameters for this love. I was forging something new. I was fifteen years old, hungry for God.

Along with this hunger, I felt the beginning of a zeal I couldn't ignore. My life was on a new trajectory that in some ways felt more natural than anything I'd known before. I wanted others to meet God as I had. I began to crave the thrill of watching a person open her eyes to a new reality. It was as if witnessing that heart-turn in another solidified that same shift in me.

Though I found this particular dimension of God—His working through me to reach others for Him—fascinatingly complex, it slowly, over time, eclipsed the fledgling simplicity of those nights that were just God and me on my back-porch swing. He had become, to me, the God who calls His people to minister. These were the verses I highlighted, the sound bites I took away from sermons. As this dimension of Him grew in my mind, it didn't leave much room to explore different sides of Him.

Just a few years later, the memories of those summer nights on the swing had faded.

I found myself in my college bedroom in an old house with stately French doors that opened to an overgrown yard. This particular day, the doors I'd rarely had time to notice were inviting. The yard seemed no longer weed infested; it was stunning. The sun breaking through the branches above formed an invitation on the fall-painted leaves.

This would have been a perfect day to open those doors (always shut), roll out my own blanket over the blanket of leaves, and fill my mind with things too big for quick consideration. My housemates and I had been delving into a Bible study that made my thoughts of Jesus linger beyond the study. It was the first time in years that I felt drawn to God in that way.

However, I reasoned, it was Sunday afternoon, the Sabbath. And to one who didn't know rest in her core, Sabbath simply meant work of a different flavor. There wasn't time on this day of Sabbath rest for things like resting.

But why? I argued with myself. *Because there are high school kids to call and Bible studies to plan.* I still had lists on this Sabbath; they just were of a ministry flavor.

Ministry is rest, isn't it?

After years of defining my Christian faith by how much and how often I poured out, my fourth year of college I was tired. That same fall, I dreamed about catching mononucleosis or some other ailment that might give me a justifiable reason to rest, deeply. My own reasons for rest—including the tiredness that had begun to set into my soul—apparently weren't enough. I needed something to force me to go there.

I was convinced that because the world around me was full of people who didn't yet know Jesus, whose hearts needed to be won, I had to meet their needs. But that outward pouring also served a different purpose. It masked me, the one who wasn't quite ready to be uncovered before the God-man I'd said yes to years before. This is really what kept me from picnicking on what I still remember to be the most beautiful fall day of my college years.

I watched that day from my window. French doors closed.

Some memories reflect our forming and some memories form us still: I stood on a stage, all fiftysomething pounds of my seven-year-old self spotlighted. I'd finished my audition song and was waiting for the voices to break through the pitch-black theater.

"So, can ya dance?" bellowed the show's director.

Up from within my bony frame came my confident reply: "Yep!"

Of course, I'd never known a dance lesson as I stood under

those big white lights. But my daddy had told me that I could do anything. So I could.

My daddy—who hiked the Grand Canyon on a whim with nothing but a Diet Coke in his hand and who created my very first memory as he flew me over that canyon in the prop-plane he copiloted on that same trip—filled my childhood with strong words.

He cracked open the sky for me.

I didn't know fear or limits. Then.

Then came the day when I pedaled home from my best friend Laura's house during the wisp of a summer between junior high and high school. I found him on the couch, slumped in pain. Man down—my invincible daddy was wounded.

One doctor's appointment gone awry, one false move, altered the course of his life.

Forever.

My dad, a coach, spent a fall that was normally jam-packed with tennis tournaments and back-to-school activities on a bed we moved into our family room. He couldn't walk the stairs. Coach Welter was out for what we hoped was just a season. It turned into years. And it took with it that little girl on the stage who could do anything.

When my dad's body broke and his back gave way, my heart went too. The man who had told me I could do anything couldn't get out of bed for months. He walked the rest of his life with a shadow over his once-vigorous existence. His words of confidence lost their weight alongside his broken story, and I received an early seed that later sprouted a question: Is God good *to me?*

So I did, then, what human nature tells us to do. I filled

in the gap between what I once knew — how I knew things should be — and this new reality. I compensated.

I moved from hair in the wind, sunshine whipping through my carefree spirit to coloring carefully within the lines. I grew cautious, craving an order that verged on rigid. I called this "measured." I drew boundary lines for myself with consequences. I called this "discipline." I moved from innocent zest and fearlessness to self-protection. I called this "maturity."

I wrapped my new patterns around myself, familiarity in an unfamiliar world.

I graduated from college and that French door home, but not from the pace I had kept there. I remember one morning as I sat in the kitchen nook of the post-college apartment I shared with a friend, with my Bible and prayer list spread out in front of me, my eyes glazed. The names on that list held stories in which I was invested and represented people I loved, yet something felt stone cold within me as I recited their names in my head as prayers, and thought, *What really is prayer anyway?* Their faces rolled through my mind like ticker tape. Check. Next name, check.

I watched the clock.

My unspoken rule was that this set-aside time, my "quiet time," as I called it, should be at least thirty minutes, but, thankfully, no more than an hour. It was a rare day when I wasn't counting down time. Life was too full with ministry to high school and college students and the community that enclosed them. I had no off button, no space apart from all this output. My mind felt like the floor of the New York

Stock Exchange. *How do you press pause on this level of activity?* I thought.

And this designated time to press toward Him, to receive? Most days it was, to me, dry obligation.

He was there and I was here and, though I spent my days telling others about Him, most of my repertoire was memories. He'd intersected my life profoundly when I was fifteen, in a forever life-altering way, but how long could the fuel from that night burn?

Sitting at the kitchen table that morning, I remembered a conversation I had with my roommate in college. I'd been propped on the dorm-room bed when I asked her, "Don't you wish you could just lump all of your time with God into one afternoon, at the beginning of the week, so you could make sure you got it done?" In other words, "Don't you wish you could just get it over with?" I could still see her frozen expression. She paused and drew in her breath, almost in disbelief that the fervent person with whom she'd lived had that line of reasoning going on inside of her. Her response signaled that what I'd shared, looking for sympathy, was not exactly the common understanding of spending time with God.

But my out-loud thinking betrayed what I lived. God was big enough for me to pattern my time into telling others about Him, but not real enough for me to find any delight in Him. He was a task, a box to be checked. The carefree little girl I once was didn't ride her bike with hands off the handlebars anymore. She was measured, careful. She was here to "do" for God.

It was as if somewhere in the recesses of my mind I believed that if I kept pouring out externally, I wouldn't need to face any internal rifts in my heart. The disconnect between who

God had made me to be and who I was becoming in order to please Him — to do this Christian life as I believed He'd ordained — was subconscious, but I made a pattern out of not addressing it. My concept of God and of following Him was creating enough flurry to hide what was broken inside.

Growth, to me, wasn't in; it was up and out. I didn't know that my insides were designed to reach and press and expand, just like I didn't know that there were sides of God I'd barely noticed. I thought I knew who He is and what His purpose is for His people. The great mystery of faith seemed a one-time decision, not a lifetime unfolding.

But this emptiness, this version of barrenness, was serving a purpose.

Soon enough I might feel so hollow, have such longing, that I would crave life. Soon enough I might recognize that God had more for me. Soon enough I would have desire.

Amid this flurry of service to God that lingered post-college, I found myself a partner who was also zeroed in on making Him known to those who didn't yet know Him. We were foisted onto a team together, reaching out to kids from the same high school.

Nate was everything I was not. He was unfiltered and spontaneous in a way that might, at times, bleed into care-lessness. I was cautious, with a heavy filter, in a way that was almost impenetrable for a "feeling" person. Where I hesitated, he sprang. We did share one major thing in common, and at this stage of life that one thing — a zeal for ministry — was my *only* thing. Nonetheless, I kept my distance from this guy for fear he might distract me from my purposed life.

Unfortunately for me at the time, some feelings I just couldn't harness. One afternoon, I had one of those rare moments alone to process the growing whirlwind of feelings for Nate I couldn't seem to keep down. This was one of the first times in my adult existence when I couldn't will myself to stop something. I escaped to a lake near the foot of the Blue Ridge Mountains to get my head straight.

I needed to ask God about this.

I sat with my open-ended question and my Bible, expecting an echo. I'd gotten used to talking at God; a mutual exchange was unfamiliar. But I was desperate to quell these feelings I'd deemed inappropriate. I couldn't see how a relationship at this stage in my life would do anything but hinder what God had "called" me to do in reaching those who didn't yet know Him.

God came, tender, touching the heart I didn't know was hard until it felt His fingertips.

He led me to Genesis 2:25, in a way I'd not known "leading" recently but quickly understood as outside of me. "They were naked and unashamed."

A verse I blushed to read hinted of a secret that, when it moved off the page and into my reality, might unravel a life-long stunted perspective on God.

I came expecting a strategy for extracting myself from a circumstance I'd labeled distracting. I left with a phrase that reverberated from His Spirit, within, to my heart: *You will marry Nate.*

I had spent years in a desert, familiar with its dryness and assuming it was just part of what it means to be a follower of Jesus, but in that desert came a drop of water. I'd squelched almost every emotion in the name of focus. Emotions were unnecessary to me. When this dewdrop fell onto my parched heart, however, thirst arose.

Could it really be His voice? He didn't give me more people to seek out for Him. He didn't impart strategies for advancing His kingdom. He didn't download my next talk or lesson or some cross-reference in Scripture.

What He offered was permission to feel, to love.

And so ensued the waterfalls.

I cried nearly every day for a month.

Years of tears, stored up, were given license for release. Some days they came out of angst; I couldn't believe the partner God had chosen for me. *Nate? Really, God?* Other days I had a looming sense that this nudge from God meant the end of living in that one-bedroom apartment I'd decided I'd know my whole lifetime. Nate was everything I worked so hard not to be. He was unbridled. It was as if I knew that joining myself to Nate meant I couldn't stay who I was or where I was.

At the time, all I knew was that Christianity (as I'd configured it) was work, and the pool of energy that I had to give had already been allotted. Where was there room for anything else?

That month was exhilarating. I began to understand that the decision I'd made as a teenager had taken me on a path of both death and life. My growing desire for Nate introduced a hunger for that life that gave me a new, though subtle, willingness to walk through death to get there. Somehow I knew, through the deluge of tears, that marriage—abandon—might fulfill the yes I'd given to God years before.

Nate would witness both the beginning of me and the end of me. His hands would hold my new understandings of God, freshly birthed, as if he were cupping our infant. And having our lives merge as they did when we were young and immature would incite a death in me of which he and God, alone, would know the intimacies. Nate would both cradle and kill.

For this union to grow, it would require the end of calcified ways of seeing God, myself, and others, and call forth from within me beauty and perspective and perseverance I had no idea were there. I couldn't articulate this, then, but something inside of me knew it.

Nate was a signpost: the new was coming, on the heels of the old dying. I was familiar with hunger once. I would be hungry for newness once again.

For Your Continued Pursuit

John 17:24–25 | 2 Corinthians 5:17 | Galatians 2:20 | Matthew 5:6 | Song of Solomon 1:4 | Genesis 2:25 | Jeremiah 29:11 | 2 Corinthians 4:16 | Ephesians 3:16–19 | Psalm 42:1 | John 4:14 | Isaiah 55:1 | Psalm 42:7 | Song of Solomon 8:6 | Proverbs 20:27 | John 15:13 | 2 Corinthians 1:21–22 | Colossians 3:10

three

NOT MY TYPICAL PRAYER

"Let me see your face, let me hear your voice."

New life rarely comes without pain. Five days after the wedding rice had been swept from the floor, I felt not hungry but empty. The emotions of our courtship, the intense sprint through our five-month engagement, and the ongoing responsibilities of leading a ministry had left me flat. I had just said a life-altering yes to Nate, but with bags under my eyes, and a weary body.

Early in our honeymoon, I spent my time lying by the pool with my Bible open on my lap and my eyelids drooping shut. I felt a growing, though still vague, discomfort with where I was and who I was, and with the fact that sleep was more appealing to me than engaging with God's Word.

Here I lay on vacation for nearly two weeks with nothing but time, and that time was disconcerting to me. With no one to minister to, I didn't know what to do with God or how to come before him without any time limitations. I was awkward with Him, as if on a wedding night, unsure of how the two of us should be around each other now that the crowds had gone home.

These were supposed to be the happiest days of my life, and I was too tired, dazed, lost to receive them. What had been starved on the inside to produce this exhaustion?

39

I had a growing sense that the problem was me. It wasn't that God was the hard driver. It was that I was driving myself and calling it God. There was a disconnect between who He really is and who I'd made Him out to be, and all the activity kept me from acknowledging that disconnect. Until now.

I had just said yes to a life of husband and wife, unaware of how that covenant might work its way into my understanding not just of Nate or myself but of God. Marriage would both undo me and rebuild me. Another circumstance might have yielded the same results, but God chose marriage, as the first of many events in my life, to spark my end and new beginning. Nate and I would find death and life in those rings and those vows, which were too big for us then and now.

All of this was happening without my buy-in. I acknowledged weak hunger pain, but that was the extent of my participation.

Despite the restlessness that crept into my honeymoon thinking, I returned home to do life exactly as I'd been doing it before.

Just weeks after our wedding, we had an opportunity to take a handful of high school kids to hear a worship concert. It was ministry, so I readily agreed.

The auditorium was thick with enthusiasm and expectation. I felt out of place in this venue; I was used to observing concerts, not participating in them, but I could tell that this crowd was ready to engage. People came full of expression, even before the music started.

The focus on worship was unfamiliar to the few souls I had brought, too. They knew concerts and sporting events and rallying places, but many of them were fresh to faith in God. Such a loud, intense gathering for praising God was new to them.

The lights were low enough for me to take in the surroundings amid the teenage flutter around me. At that time in my life, anything outside of my paradigm of Christianity fell prey to my evaluation. And this display of music, dance, and preaching was on the edges of what I considered familiar.

I was a driver that night, ushering these high school kids to the place where they might see God. I could do this role in my sleep—leading, guiding, shepherding—but as the music played, I started to steal fewer looks at how these ones I loved were receiving this experience. I felt something dislodge inside me.

My heart was ever so slightly moving. Rather, it was being moved. Not uncommon for a believer in Jesus, but in recent years my spiritual life had little connection with my heart.

In fact, in my experience of Christianity, my heart rarely moved except around the conversion of other hearts. A holy night when a soul saw Him for the first time was my chance for the straw by the manger to crease my knees too. I saw Him welling up in the lives of others. Their stories then became my stories, so deeply that I lost my own journey.

When others grew, I grew. I knew no other way for it to happen.

So the night of this concert was strange to me. The high school kids already knew Him, so I didn't have an opportunity for Christian "success" in the way I'd defined it. Yet I found myself moving from being stirred to being overcome. I sensed that I could stop the in-flooding of emotion, but I didn't want it to stop.

This stirring spoke to that hunger pain that crept up weeks before on my honeymoon. It lingered in the days that followed, this movement from God. Just like falling in love with Nate, it was distracting.

Days later, still only weeks after we'd said "I do," I found myself scribbling a prayer that was more of a raw asking than an item on a list: "There has to be more of You, God, than what I'm understanding. I want to know more of You." The words came from outside me, though already attached to me. This was not my typical prayer.

Later, I learned that Nate, who was buried in a mass of high school testosterone just rows ahead of me that night, was having his own private conversation. He'd witnessed an older, respected friend a few rows over from him, arms outstretched, unashamed of private worship in a public place. This guy wasn't demonstrative by nature, but apparently that night, something called for an expression that was open for others to see. Nate couldn't look away. He hadn't seen a man worship like that before, on this continent at least.

Instead of viewing his friend with a skeptical eye, Nate had this thought-turned-prayer: *He has something I don't. I want what he has.*

Nate and I unknowingly had a convergence that night, one we first identified together months later. Those simple prayers, though not flippant, were casual. They certainly weren't eloquent, but they were the beginnings of a deeper hunger—and a lifetime feast.

The entwining of lives and stories that happened on the day that I wore white and Nate's tears fell into my bouquet was beginning to take the shape of a singular love story, one much greater.

We had not yet reached our first anniversary on that mild January day in Charlottesville. My mind was oblivious to the weather, though, as I neared her office door. It was thinking, *Run and hide!* I slumped my shoulders as I opened the door to the corridor that held her office. *What did I do to get myself here?*

From my perspective, counselors were for true down-and-outers — those whose communities and belief systems couldn't fix what life had dealt. Counselors were a last resort for those beyond repair.

But I was beginning to believe that I *was* beyond repair. I couldn't even conceptualize what repair would be like. I felt a dull throbbing all over. I couldn't point to an event that instigated this kind of pain, so my natural conclusion, and fear, was that my heartsickness might be a forever sickness.

Thanksgiving had been bleak, Christmas even colder in my heart. The word *depression* crept into my mind's periphery, but I refused the label. I prayed that prayer just weeks after our honeymoon — *There has to be more of You, God, than what I'm understanding. I want to know more of You* — and now here I was plodding through each day with a lump in my throat. I couldn't understand how I could pray a prayer so big and then be forced to live in a box that felt so small. Didn't hunger provoke a feeding? I was more starved now than I had been just a few months before.

"I just can't continue to live like this, Nate," I had said, as I was swept away by the post-holiday blues that people who celebrate the birth of Jesus weren't supposed to feel.

A sadness hung like a shroud over my newlywed existence. I continued the motions of preaching Jesus to others (what else was I to do?), despite the fact that I was unable to detect Him in my own life. But the deeper I sank, the hollower my words about Him were. *Maybe if I just keep talking*, I thought, *maybe He will come.*

I didn't know how to pray and wait. I had made a big ask of Him—one I had never made before—and then resorted to living life my habitual way, with no idea what to do with the question I'd just posed.

I stayed there until "bone dry" became uncomfortable enough for me to move. So Nate and I concluded that counseling was the best option for help. And I landed at the door of a woman I'd never met, alongside a friend who agreed to sit in with me as a silent support, with an ache in my heart that said, *Somebody, anybody—help.*

I didn't know, when my fingers wrapped themselves around the handle of the glass door on that day and my head hung low in the hope I wouldn't see anyone I knew, that I was on the edge of one of the greatest awakenings of my inner life.

Hunger often looks more encumbering than holy. It seems to detract and distract from life's real ascent. The hunger that got me in the door that day didn't feel holy at all. It felt awkward and uncomfortable, like any hollowness might feel.

But holy it was.

I wasn't prepared for her questions. She asked obscure ones, seemingly unrelated to my issues.

"You're a runner? What's the longest distance you've ever run?" she asked without looking up from the legal pad on which she was noting my responses to her rapid-fire questions.

"A marathon," I said. "Last year."

"What did it feel like to train for the marathon? Did you set a time goal?" She was clearly driving at something, but I couldn't answer her question when at the same time I was analyzing where she was going. I could tell that how I answered would determine what she asked next. Choose your own adventure.

One hour later and leaving behind a file full of notes, I left with a glimmer of hope, though the hour had not at all been what I'd expected.

There was no discussion, just questions and my answers, except for one comment she made before I left. God left me a crumb—because a crumb was all I could chew at the time. "How well do you think your husband knows you?"

"Really well," I responded without thinking.

After a studied pause, she asked, "What percentage of 'all of you' does he know?"

"Eighty percent," I said confidently. We had known each other two and half years, with just more than a year of that time spent holding hands, not just brushing elbows, in ministry, and several months of being a wedded couple.

"We'll talk about this more later, but I might suggest that he knows about one percent of you. Five percent, at best. There are vast frontiers of you to be discovered that he has not yet explored."

Minutes later, she was ushering me out. I wrote her a check and scheduled my next appointment as if I were at the dentist.

I didn't realize the reverberation that that one thought—one comment by an outsider—might have in the hours, and years, to come.

I had grown to know myself and others and the world around me in binary dimensions. It wasn't as if I saw layers in Nate or myself and feared pursuing them. I'd simply never thought about it.

The counselor's words, later lingering over me, made me consider a seminal image of my childhood that Nate had never witnessed: When I was growing up, we had a swivel chair in our sunroom that I'm certain was worn soft with the imprint of my tush. My mom would find me there most days with the back of the chair toward the door and me tucked away in that little corner, face in the pages of a book.

I loved to read.

Our local children's bookstore, The Reading Railroad, was like a candy store to me. It came second only to our library. The summer our county unveiled its new library building, Nikki from up the street and I pedaled our ten-speeds there almost daily and topped off our trip with a stop at the TCBY. We'd get lost between the stacks of books and corner bean-bag chairs, breaking only for a sweet treat. The smell of new, uncracked-open pages invigorated me just about as much as the feel of the worn pages of library books.

Somewhere between the days of folding myself up in that chair and the days of owning a car that could have sliced the all-day trip to the library down to a quick dash, I decided that the love that stories stirred in me didn't contribute to my goal of being a passionate pursuer of God. So I dropped them.

Sure, I kept reading and filling my bookshelves, but I limited myself only to practical books I thought would grow my faith. Good and rich books, but not the stories that once drew me in and painted pictures on my mind.

This was a reflection of the shift my life was taking: Less time getting lost in story, more time zeroing in on what I might produce.

That was the woman Nate married. No sunroom reading chair in sight.

Nate and I had entered marriage in our early twenties. What we lacked in life experience we made up for in opinions about how life should be lived.

The honeymoon had ended before it started; our first big fight as a married couple, just a few days into "newlywed bliss," had left me walking back to our hotel by myself, by my own choice. It was a little argument—a decision about what to do the next day—but because we lacked the maturity to face the workings of our own hearts, even the smallest argument seemed to return us to that chasm between us—and the chasm between our individual hearts and God's heart.

Our move from friendship to engagement to marriage had happened in a flash. We each had attached ourselves to parts of the other one, parts we described to friends who hadn't yet seen us together.

"He loves seeing high school kids come to know Jesus," I'd say. "He wants to do full-time ministry for the rest of his life, too."

"She's a born leader," he'd say with pride.

Not only did we define ourselves by our output, we defined each other that way too. I loved how Nate pursued evangelism, and I saw his faith in light of the lives he might touch in his lifetime. I noticed his heart for those who were "lost." I praised him for the line behind him of lives that he had influenced.

At one point while we were dating, Nate mentioned his stint across Europe in his college days and the art museums where he'd spent hours. His music collection held classical composers he loved—scratched CDs from his childhood home. When we started to join our stuff, as the representation of lives being joined, I remember vaguely noticing stacks of poetry books. But few of these things came to mind when I considered Nate. They were negligible details about his life that didn't fit within our narrow focus on ministry. I discarded them, just as I had discarded parts of my own life.

I'm certain I never told Nate about all those years I spent buried in books. I'd never mentioned that my favorite Christmas memory is that every year my parents would let me stay up, reading, as late as I wanted on Christmas Eve. I had dismissed those parts of my past as insignificant parts of me as well.

So when, not long into marriage, I discovered that Nate made space in his schedule for things I considered needless, I grew irritated. Things like reading novels and going fishing and attending the symphony were a waste of time to me. There were souls to save, lives to win for Jesus. How did a cello fit into that?

I'd been successful at managing my life, making sure there were no colors outside of the lines. Now I had another life, pushed up against mine, that I assumed was mine to manage.

I monitored him, as best could a woman married to a strong man who valued his independence. I made feeble attempts to convince him that my narrow way was *our* way and *God's* way and the *only* way.

Naturally, he bristled. Who wouldn't?

Round and round we went, me determined to steer our course and Nate determined to be his own man, and I didn't always like how he chose to do that.

Externally it appeared to be the conflict of two stubborn leaders who couldn't bend for the other. Internally, there was another pursuit.

That little girl in pigtails with books stashed in her backpack—pedaling faster on the way home from the library than she did on the way there because she couldn't wait to stick her nose in the pages—was as much who I was as the woman with a zeal to see lives changed. God had led me to a man who might, one day, clasp my hand and visit with me the parts of myself I'd long squelched. And He had brought Nate a woman who would, one day, do the same for him.

More of You, God, Nate and I had prayed together, apart, that concert night. It wasn't just the beginning of unraveling our understanding of Him. It began the unraveling of our understanding of ourselves.

I began to crack open the books, his, that I had put into boxes to give away once he no longer missed them. I wept the first time we went to the symphony. And I remembered he had been an English major the year I started to write.

But that counselor's question incited another question in me: If there was more to me and more to Nate—more to us— could it be, also, that my version of God was limited?

If my complexity was exponentially greater than I'd assessed, what did that say of the One who made me?

Could there be more to Him?

The weak plea I'd made to Him early in my marriage would lead to a death. But death was necessary for this prayer to be answered. To find Him, I had to let go of me. Or rather, let go of the me I had designed so carefully over the years. The hardest part would be letting go not just in front of God but alongside the human husband who was himself learning to let go.

For Your Continued Pursuit

Romans 5:3–5 | Romans 8:28 | Ephesians 1:17–19 | Colossians 1:9–12 | Psalm 42:2 | Psalm 63:1 | John 6:35 | 1 Samuel 16:7 | Psalm 8:3–8 | 1 John 3:1–2

four

LOOKING LONG

"For He has torn, but He will heal us."

We stood in the kitchen of the building where our new church was meeting, talking casually about a topic that was anything but casual for me. Newly married and facing the reality that marriage had meant an emotional detour from the "ascent" I'd expected in God, I was ripe for insight from another. She had been married for nearly two decades and had a history from which to draw. As she removed plastic wrap from casseroles and put serving spoons in dips and dressings, I wondered whether she could read my confusion on the topic.

Socially aware enough to know that the most personal struggles in marriage are not to be shared with just anyone, I divulged little but absorbed much. I was hoping for anything that might help. Then she told me, laughing in the way you do after you've been through pain you'll likely not revisit in the same way, that the first ten years of her marriage were hard. *Ten years? You have got to be kidding me*, I thought. *I am barely treading water after a few months, and you're telling me this could last for ten years?*

Nate and I were in full-time ministry together, on a small team with others, "reaching the world" for Jesus in a parachurch organization. What had slung us together just a few years before—a passion and love for seeing hardened teenage hearts soften under the truth of the gospel—was now where many of our conflicts concentrated.

I was drawn to Nate's intensity. He threw all of himself into what he loved, and since he loved what I loved—these "long gone" teenagers revitalized by a relationship with Jesus—I was attracted to him all the more. But as we pursued this shared heart, the differences in our angle of approach only grew more pronounced.

Our small team spent late nights dreaming about how God might use us to change the world. Expectation of God's outward work through us and passion about our vision filled our hearts. Fun, of the crazy kind, was a prerequisite in the midst of pouring our lives out into high school and college kids. But it was "ministry" fun. We left little time for much else.

Impact was our currency. Yet neither Nate nor I had considered reverse impact—God impacting us, the kind of impact that happens behind closed doors. Neither of us was prepared to change, to die, for the other.

At times I naively wished for what I had assumed was the greatest conflict most married couples face: whether to squeeze the toothpaste from the top or bottom.

Our conflicts felt weightier than any anecdote I'd heard, and they had begun to meld, all of them. Did the conflict start yesterday over the fact that he wasn't following up on the connection for our fall fundraiser the way I would, or was he annoyed with how I responded to his attempts to connect with me in the middle of my workday?

Our arguments uncovered wounds deep enough that it was easier to walk painstakingly around areas that might create conflict than to address them.

During one of our worst fights, I declared things that most

people would have the self-control only to think and then dismiss. Venomous words spilled out of my mouth as if they were casual assessments. I couldn't stop myself.

Who have I become? Or is this who I've been all along and it's finally breaking the surface?

I spoke as if I wanted him to leave. I convinced myself that I wanted him to leave. I wanted him to confirm what I already believed: that I wasn't worth "sticking it out" for.

The rule follower I'd become had also, regularly—mostly subconsciously—held me to a standard I would never meet. I was constantly working toward a goal that was impossible for my humanity to achieve and punishing myself for not reaching it. If Nate just left, then I would feel sufficiently punished.

These thoughts about myself were new to me. They had lingered for so long in the background that I never would have identified myself as one who lived with shame or insecurity. But the distance between my inner life and my outward living for God was revealing itself. It had taken something, someone, to show it to me.

Before I knew it, what had been smoldering for years inside me was right in front of us. It was messy and, in many ways, unidentifiable. It hurt Nate to weather my words, and it hurt me to say them, and yet they spilled out.

That hunger I was feeling? Looking back, I see that it doesn't create the gaps in our hearts; it exposes them.

But instead of running, retreating, as I'd both hoped and feared Nate would, he wrapped his wounded self around me and held me close enough to absorb me. It was as if he had been conditioned to respond to the worst of me by leaning *in*, not away.

He whispered in my ear, "I love you. You are beautiful to

me. I forgive you, even if you don't have the words to ask for my forgiveness."

His words held a power over me.

They were fresh against my own thoughts, which were old and stale.

They breathed new life.

But all along, the overarching question through every argument, every reconciliation, hung like a question over my life: *Who is God, here?* And: *Can I trust that God knows what is best for me when He called me to marry Nate? Can I trust that He is good to me?*

As friends shared stories about travels and ministry endeavors, I felt like Nate and I were just trying to stay afloat on the tides of our hearts. I was jealous that other couples were changing the world.

Little did I know that, indeed, we *were* changing the world. God was using my husband to change my world, and me to change his. And this world changing started by exposing our deepest questions of God — to ourselves and to each other.

I had lived buttoned up, tidied, for years. Now what had been so laboriously stuffed inside of me was coming out under the safety of a covenant with a husband who was ready to hold it. The gaps in my understanding of God finally formed themselves into real-life questions. I'd been asking them all along, but I was so disconnected from my heart that I didn't realize my life wasn't a declaration about God; it was, instead, a question *of* Him.

Was God good to me? I couldn't hold that question *and* at the same time believe in the full life He offered me.

To be filled anew, I needed not just to acknowledge hunger but to recognize how necessary that hunger was. My day had come. And it was by the hand of my husband, who found his own hunger as he practiced years, not just days, of whispering, "You are beautiful to me," through the darkest parts of my life.

She called as I was on my way to the bait and tackle store.

I had left the house twenty minutes before, in anger.

Another unresolved marital conflict.

Symptoms. I was living enough of this conflict to begin to understand it. But as Nate and I made an unspoken agreement to dig into one another's mess—we just did it—it seemed as if things got worse, not better. More conflict, more rub, more pieces of our hearts awry and exposed.

We were beginning to understand that all this had a purpose. The habit of avoiding the deeper parts of our hearts, though easier at the moment, couldn't coexist with our growing desire for a new experience with God.

From my vantage point, however, it sure looked like a mess. I didn't know how to do "mess" outwardly, in the presence of others. Even those who loved me. I had lived so long tending to the outer parts of me and my faith that I had sparse understanding of how to tend to the inside, much less speak of it to another.

So when my dear college friend called to catch up on life, a year into our marriage and with Nate and I knee-deep in relational muck, I answered the phone out of resignation. I wanted the most recent nuptial fire to smolder before I had to answer, "So what's going on?" but the cooling period hadn't happened. If I kept avoiding phone calls until I had a few days without a war of words in my home, it might mean forever living on an island.

So here I was, days before Nate's birthday, on the way to pick up the fishing pole I had, after much research, settled on for his gift. This fishing pole was my olive branch, an affirmation of his love of a sport that I saw as unnecessary in the pursuit of Christ and lost souls. A reminder that I still held hope.

But I wasn't sure my friend on the other end of the phone line would understand. We chatted and I spoke a little of where I was in my heart. I tried her out but, out of awkwardness, didn't give her a fair opportunity. I was not versed in how to talk about the level of pain Nate and I were facing. While she could have been doing the same kind of hiding I was, our brief conversation revealed that none of her plates had been smashed and no chairs broken. My first year of marriage was explosive. Hers seemed peaceful. I quickly ruled her out as one who could step into my world and help make sense of it, or at least hold my hand through it.

I was bearing up under an ache I believed only a few could know. I had to hide it, because who could understand it?

I was beginning to think that each of us on this earth falls into a category of cursed or blessed and that my outward circumstances were starting to tell the story: I was cursed. She, obviously, was blessed.

So we talked about her vacation and my ministry.

When I arrived at the bait and tackle store, I deposited the tissues from my front seat into the trash can outside and told my girlfriend that I had to go. I left her thinking things were fine, but I wished I could live in that saccharine world of how others saw me.

Is this God's best for me? rang in my ears.

When I met God at fifteen, I believed (without realizing it) that living Christianity well meant being reborn once and then growing—upward and outward.

My marriage and the husband whom God gave me were ushering me into a new reality. I was going down, not up. In, not out. But God wasn't turning His head from my falling. He was near. My gaps and Nate's gaps were not a threat to Him. They were an invitation. I had asked for *more of You, God*, and that meant more of me exposed. I was fumbling to get my arms around the reality that my exposure—to Nate, to God, even to a friend on the other end of my phone—wasn't to be feared. It was holy.

When I was fifteen and under the blanket of that winter sky, *this* was what I had said yes to.

My love for the beach was now something to share with Nate, a part of me shyly emerging and wanting him to follow.

My dad first taught me to love the ocean. The smell of saltwater is synonymous to me with the smell of his skin. Despite the fact that 358 days of the year we were hundreds of miles away from the shore, our annual week at the water left an impact that almost became my singular impression of my father.

My dad inhaled the ocean air and could sit on the end of the deck and watch the waves for hours. The beach was also his place to slow down and experience the small things. He noticed the sand crabs. The colors of light on the water. He was witness to all that the ocean held with or without him to watch.

My most memorable moments with my dad, other than long talks on our stiff living room furniture away from the hub of activity in our everyday house, were of the sun setting on our freckled bodies as we clung to the rafts that kept us afloat. The waves were as tall as he was in my memory.

My dad wasn't afraid of things unknown, uncontrollable. Places like the Swiss Alps and the Grand Canyon, fraught with angles that would never be fully explored, were invitations to him. My dad taught me that there are some mysteries worth throwing all of yourself into pursuing until they become familiar. The beach was a place to dream.

"One more, Daddy! Just one more wave!" kept us riding waves right up until dinner. My dad came alive at the ocean, that one week of the year, and he spent the other fifty-one weeks planning for the next trip. He left me a legacy beyond sand castles.

Every year, my feet refound their home in the sand. Every year, a new part of me that wasn't new at all, just stowed away, emerged at the ocean. The cadence of the waves—both when the sun was hot overhead and when it was slipping away to make room for the moon—brought with it a slew of memories akin to those I'd made on my back-porch swing that first summer after I'd said yes to Jesus. In reality, it may have been only a few weeks of nights that I spent on that swing, but the scent of the God I'd encountered there was pungent enough to make it feel like I'd lived a decade in that one summer.

The beach had that same musk. The little girl with pigtails whipping in the wind was accessible to me there, no matter how driven I had been in the weeks and months leading up to that time. The little girl who used to be carefree and trusting. The little girl who didn't wear a watch.

The first year Nate and I went to the beach as a married couple allowed me to have a dialogue that wasn't just internal. At the time, our marriage, like the ocean, was both great and terrible. We had horrific arguments and late-night confessions, often in the same wave of self-protection and self-discovery.

That week we enjoyed being with each other and with my family. We took long bike rides and sank our chairs into the sand and read books until the tide came up underneath us. We walked the beach for hours and spent our nights on rocking chairs listening to graying fiftysomethings relive their youth as they sang their own renditions of Beach Boys songs in harborside cafes.

We breathed.

It was in the midst of this inhalation that I noted the state of my heart—again. It was as if I needed to weave in and out of the same new understanding of myself many times, in many different scenarios, before I got it.

The hunger that had surfaced on my honeymoon and then weeks later at the concert began to gnaw again. It had appeared when I felt the pain of emotions inside of me spilling over my marriage. It had come when I was void of all feeling amid a life I'd claimed as being purposed for God.

And it came when life slowed to a stop at the beach. It was becoming hard to ignore.

I had once thought hunger is just for those who don't yet have a personal relationship with Jesus. But I was growing to know hunger as the undercurrent of the life that comes *after* saying yes to Him.

This particular week, my mind saw what my heart had been feeling. The God I'd constructed from pieces of Scripture and teachings and personal experience was not satisfying me. Years of striving, trying to get Him not only to notice me but to approve of me, had worn me thin.

"This can't be right," I said to Nate early one evening as

we revisited the ocean, now placid and free of the hundreds of children who had been there earlier in the day. "This can't be all He has for me, to live this way and under this pressure."

I remembered out loud the prayer I'd prayed days after the concert. It had become a signpost for us, this request for something more.

At the same time that I acknowledged my emptiness those months before, I had begun to meet others who wore a brand of Christianity that was attractive, but foreign, to me. In retrospect, it seems orchestrated by God that our everyday circles had broadened enough to bring in a few additional friends of various ages who, individually, pursued God in a way that felt like they were a collective whole. Some of them didn't even know one another. But they all shared something in common. They acted as if they believed God didn't just tolerate them; He enjoyed them. And yet their messes were more visible than mine. I couldn't understand this combination, but it intrigued me. They lived and walked as if they knew God was good to them, though their circumstances said otherwise. These people liked to pray, and they referenced their day-to-day experience with God as if it were an adventure.

What did this smattering of friends have that I didn't? Expectation. They approached their days with a confidence that God had something for them—not just one big something but lots of little somethings. She wanted to hear God during the morning carpool and commune with Him in the front seat while childhood chatter rose in the back seat. He interrupted his work that hid him behind a computer all day to take walks and talk with God. All of them had everyday anecdotes that spoke of relational encounters with God that I didn't know.

I'd had my fill of the version of God I was following. But these friends were still hungry.

Nate and I continued to chew on our hunger for hunger, until the sun began to set over the ocean. These were the everyday moments my dad had taught me to ponder by pondering them himself. Even years of narrowing my focus to "impact" and "intentionality" in faith hadn't broken the habit I'd learned from him.

We stopped to watch. When I saw the sun's final rays painting the water an electric amber, something lifted in me.

I *felt*. Not the torrent I'd once struggled to hold down but the release of something from Him into a place inside of me. This moment was more than effort. I was receiving.

The word *glory* dropped into my mind as my heart caught in my throat. *Glory* wasn't in my vocabulary, but this event, which had happened every single day of my life up until now, was laced with something new.

Beauty had me spellbound.

God was in this sunset.

He was near.

Before my fingers could find Nate's to squeeze and signal *this is His*, the sun-stained water exposed another display. A group of baby sand sharks formed a ring, cresting and falling below the waterline over and over again. In all my years at the beach, I'd never seen sea life like that. It was if their movements were conducted.

That evening at the beach, God was on display. That vision spoke louder to me than all the testimonies I'd heard, all the years of telling people about Jesus. For one of the first times, I saw that God wasn't just involved in my output. He wasn't investing in me *so that* I would invest in others. He was revealing Himself to me independent of what I might produce as a result of it.

Just because.

The beach wasn't deserted that night. Others pedaled their bikes past our display, pointing and smiling at what caused us to pause. What was worthy of a nod from them is an event we still talk about, here a decade later.

That small moment was grace. I didn't earn it or win it. It wasn't a prize. But I could own it. God infused a few minutes with His glory, at my most undeserving time—I was at the height of naively pursuing religious perfection—all so that I might notice that He noticed me. And so that in turn I might notice Him.

Isn't that glory? Seeing His reflection across our sin-stained existence and, in turn, looking long at Him with our lives?

And isn't that love? Turning to another and looking long?

For Your Continued Pursuit

Romans 8:1 | John 4:13–14 | 1 Corinthians 2:9 | Proverbs 3:5–6 | Psalm 16:7 | Psalm 18:28–30 | Isaiah 58:11 | Revelation 22:17 | 2 Corinthians 4:16 | Psalm 51:6 | Psalm 143:6 | Zephaniah 3:17 | 1 Thessalonians 5:16–18 | 2 Corinthians 3:18 | Psalm 19:1–6 | Romans 11:36 | Colossians 1:27

five

I BARELY KNOW YOU

"For My thoughts are not your thoughts."

I sat straight up in bed. It was still the middle of the night, but I couldn't shake the dream from which I'd awakened.

In the dream, I had died and the world kept going as I watched from a perch. I witnessed my funeral, but not the songs sung or the faces of those who attended or the flowers. Just one eulogy.

The girl speaking in the dream was one in whom—in real life—I'd invested my time and my late-night prayers over the years. At the time that I had the dream, she was no longer in high school, but her adolescent years had made an impression not just on her but on me. She was that wild-spirited high school kid to whom I'd had the honor, years earlier, of telling about Jesus, and with whom I'd held hands through the dozens of times she wanted to turn away from the yes she had given Him.

I can still remember her teenage face and her locked-in stare as I talked with her for the first time about this God who isn't distant, but who is near enough to offer Himself for her. A heart like this one—so enmeshed in the glitz of the world around her and successful enough by its standards not to appear to have need—was exactly the kind of heart I prayed He would change. My fast-paced ministry life had a face behind it then, and it was hers: the thick-skinned high school girl who had a knack for hiding her deep need even as she desperately wanted someone to see it.

In my dream I reasoned that it was only natural that she was the one speaking at my funeral. She was my legacy.

Her role in my dream was short, just as the dream itself was. She made no mention of my impact on her life. Her eulogy was brief and pointed and had nothing to do with her. She stood up at that dream service and said, "The most significant thing about Sara's life is that she held the key to Nate's heart."

Those words have lingered with me from the moment I woke to them. They later became an encouragement, but when I first heard them, they were a correction. I had developed a habit of freely pouring love into the unlovely outside of my home. I had little left for the one with whom I'd linked arms to change the world. My concept of love wasn't broad enough to consider my participation in the changing of *his* world.

It was easier to love in the public eye, when I knew I might not be the only witness of God's love touching another's heart. But to love Nate, behind the closed doors of our home and the sealed doors of his heart, required something I didn't yet have.

God didn't bring us together just for Nate's strong arms to hold me when I was dark. I too carried a love that would unlock his heart. But it was a love I couldn't muster, a love that sometimes felt far from natural. This love that God would conduct through me required an infusion of Himself. It required loving Nate in the face of the dark parts of him, just as he'd loved me when my darkest angles were exposed.

Marriage would be the first of many times to come when I needed to love in a way that reflected a characteristic of God that was yet unfamiliar to me.

Nate and I weren't there just to witness the flesh of one another die. We were part of love's rebuilding in the other.

"I get to be the one," Nate said as he held me in the kitchen, his arms wrapped tightly around my back.

That afternoon in the kitchen, he still dripping with sweat from the morning's workout and I with eyes bloodshot from crying, he spoke a phrase that was our banner. He labeled the season, which may very well have been the label of our lives. I was a mess and he wasn't running away. He was leaning in.

"I get to be the one who sees the story, up close," he whispered in my ear, though there was no one there to hear it. It felt too holy to say loudly. "I get to be the one who knows the story behind the story. I get to see the real treasure in you."

Those words weren't too far from the words that had emerged from the mouth of the Father over the years I'd felt I was living in the dark. He not only saw me when the lights were off, but He knew me. And God loved the sincerity that He saw. The years that were beginning to feel like a wash—externally unproductive, as my insides were being exposed with the intent to heal—were His treasure. I'd let Him in, and this was His delight. Yes, buried in my mess, He found treasure. In me.

Though this was only just the beginning, God was giving me new life out of the hunger that He'd carved.

God too said the words He felt toward me: "I get to be the One."

My mess wouldn't forever be a curse. One day it would be my crown. One day it would tell the story that, yes, He is good ... to me.

Three years into marriage, we needed a temporary place to stay between living in our newlywed shanty and moving into the first home we would own. Friends told us about a farm and the family who owned it and their little attached cottage, newly vacant. Perfect.

We had acquired entirely too much stuff for this one-bedroom interim stay, but even the six months we were there was long enough to elicit homemaking. Home it became. In fact, home was reoriented around Chinquapin Hill Farm. We had a few hundred square feet to ourselves on its sixty acres, and that was just enough.

Chinquapin was our sunroom, a greenhouse for our growth. While our eyes were set on what would come next, we were changing inside. This farm and its inhabitants became much more to us than summer camp.

In just the first day of unpacking, we went from acquaintances to confidants with our host family's children, in a way that only preadolescent years can welcome. They spread themselves across the couch and that old chair I just couldn't part with for our short stint there while we waited for our house to be ready. We watched with disguised curiosity how this melded family worked.

One child from Romania, another from Russia, between three lanky-like-their-father siblings who knew nothing other than family as a melting pot. They fought like they shared a womb and loved one another's quirks in a way that made me wish I too had been grafted in for longer than just a summer.

"I think this is more than just a place to stay," I whispered to Nate that first night, uncertain of how thick the walls were in that hundred-year-old farmhouse. We listened to crickets that we assumed were outside but could very well have been sharing the same creaky bed with us, the same bed that cradled their grandmother's passing, years before.

Everything at Chinquapin had a story, and Chinquapin had a story for us.

In the summer, when insulation and heat were not an issue, farm life was romantic. But it wasn't just the farm. Even deeper than the allure of the big sky over that acreage at the base of the Blue Ridge Mountains was what God was speaking to us. It wasn't loud. It was a voice weaving its way into our normal. He was making His heaven-sent plans a reality we'd soon settle into.

"You think?" Nate said, curious, not skeptical.

"Yep," I said. "There's something for us here."

In a way only God can do, He was infusing the everyday with the supernatural, a simple conversation with a lifelong vision.

It was obvious we were transitioning from one home to another, but a less obvious transition was also happening in our hearts. This family and the blending of their stories would play into the new life God was going to bring forth out of our soon-discovered barrenness.

"I think we're going to adopt," I said. My words broke through the cricket songs peppering another muggy night on the farm.

"I know," said Nate. "Me too."

My hunger was becoming something I welcomed. I'd gone from certainty about who God is and how He works to a subtle whisper I prayed, often: *I barely know You.*

And He whispered back, *Here's more.*

He knew my question—the one that had newly emerged yet would continue to surface throughout my story—and He was responding.

As I wrestled to expand my view of God, whom I had known as coach, teacher, and instructor, Nate and I received an offer of extravagant goodness. An offer I resisted with everything in me.

A gift from a friend enabled us to build a new home in our community. It was an excessive, unexpected gift, the one that had landed us on the farm while we waited for its completion.

The first time we drove around looking at lots and considering floor plans, I wanted to vomit. I, the girl who had spent much of her adult life ashamed of the fact that she noticed things like good quality towels and natural-stone floor tile, was given an opportunity to "shop."

From my perspective, the true believer was to be a minimalist in both quantity and quality. Jesus' instructions to sell your possessions and give to the poor trumped any picture of God-given extravagance to be found in Scripture. Money was dangerous. Like a number of things I'd placed in its category, it was to be avoided, entirely.

This gift threatened the paradigm I'd nursed for most of my Christian life.

It wasn't too long into picking floor stains and wall colors and light fixtures that it dawned on me: my struggle was not about the house; it was about my perspective on God.

I was still inside the tension of loving our new home and wrestling with whether our hearts would eventually grow cold as a result of it when I walked a friend through the rooms we were unpacking. Clearly we had more space than the two of us needed. But the details of this gift were not to be divulged. I knew I couldn't tell the story. The internal work God was doing required my external silence. For all our friends may have perceived, this was the dream house we'd been angling for our whole lives.

This friend with whom I'd spent hours, regularly, poring over the Bible and teaching her what I understood to be God's truths clearly couldn't understand this disconnect. *How did they sell out?* she must have been thinking. *They've diverged from living the gospel.* I knew, regrettably, that those would have been my thoughts just a year before. I knew that I'd judged others who were living in homes like the one we now lived in.

I was embarrassed—both for who I had been then and for who I appeared to be now.

On another afternoon, I unpacked my third bedroom while on the phone with a long-distance friend who was ranting about friends of hers who had a home "way bigger" than what they needed, as if she couldn't believe they could be followers of God *and* have that house. I had subscribed to her thinking. I had said her words, years earlier, yet here I was with an extravagant gift that was forcing me out of my old ways of thinking about money even as it forced me out of stale and limited ways of seeing God.

"Uh-hm," I said, lacking confidence to speak about this nascent understanding of Him that had been stirring inside of me as I moved into this "way bigger than I needed" house.

This was more about His story in me, I realized, than it was about the house. All those young adult years when I had patterned my life to squelch creativity had also squelched the God of the creative. Now I could no longer deny God's extravagance. I hid the gift of our house as long as I could, panicked my way through receiving it, and yet marveled at a side of God I'd never before known.

I knew I didn't deserve this. I didn't feel I could be trusted with it. But God wasn't sitting back, fearful that I would suddenly cash in on this gift as a lifestyle and become a spendthrift instead of a fervent follower of Him. He wanted to show me Himself as the Father who gives gifts to His children. This scenario wasn't setting me up for materialism; it was deconstructing my misconception of Him as a tightfisted Father, someone who is concerned only with my getting life "right."

God was spoiling me, the child who'd confined herself to one small room of Him but was hungering for more. He was revealing Himself as extravagant. Uncomfortably extravagant. He was showing me what I would need to know about Him when we faced the season ahead. Because this display of His extravagance would fade compared with the extravagance He would offer me, in Himself—alone—when my body revealed itself as barren.

And so we moved into a beautiful new house with this burgeoning perspective on Him.

But we still didn't know I could not bear children.

I remember one evening soon after our move when Nate and I came across the story behind that old hymn "It Is Well with My Soul." While many others grew up with hymns like this ringing through their heads, it was new to me.

We sat in our upstairs office that we were sure would one day be a baby's room, I in the comfy chair and Nate at the desk reading to me the hymn's background that he'd found online. Though not expecting, we were full of expectation for our lives.

At that moment we'd had what we thought was hardship, but which, in retrospect, was only a practice run for harder days ahead. We chafed alongside one another's wounds and we were bruised, but not battered. Marriage felt hard, nearly impossible at times, but God had been circling those moments with new revelations of Himself. The hard and the good *were* intertwined. We had had enough "hard" that we could naively say that this chapter in our lives was over and done with, never to be revisited.

Even so, our life's coming sting resounded in the birth story of this hymn. It was one Nate had sung many times, but even he had forgotten that the words were penned by a man whose heart had been torn open by the loss of all of his children.

"Saved alone" were the words written on the telegram that Anna Spafford wrote to her husband, Horatio, after their four daughters were killed in a shipwreck crossing the Atlantic Ocean to England. As Nate read to me the story and we listened to the hymn this father wrote in response, something welled up inside of me. I didn't know, then, that it was a foreshadowing—even a promise—but I was stirred. Nate in the desk chair and me in the recliner beside it, arms folded over my chest, in silence, listening. We both fought tears as if in some way we knew this night was ominous.

The words Horatio Spafford wrote were the anthem I craved, even when life felt only stretched, not snapped:

Whatever my lot, Thou has taught me to say,
"It is well, it is well with my soul."

I read the words. I sang the words. My mind danced over what produced this perspective in the face of such great loss. This song, and its story, told of God's ways. It spoke of fruit in a life I didn't understand and exposed layers of a God I'd never experienced myself or even examined in Scripture.

I often pictured the future from the perspective of fear, as if imagining the worst-case scenario might allow me to prepare myself. But God comes kindly to prepare, and with a grace He'll release only in that moment, not in advance.

That night His kindness gave Nate and me those words and that story as an aspiration. We wanted what God offered us before we knew what we might have to walk through to get it.

Spafford was one of many people — authors, pastors, poets — lined up across my timeline whose stories carried the scent of an alluring, an intimacy with God beyond circumstances. Each breathed a connection to a God who was foreign to me but resonated with something deep inside me. It was as if I were an adopted child meeting a biological sibling who introduced me to our Father for the first time. He was familiar, we were connected, yet I didn't know Him like they did.

I wanted to have the deep parts of me find the deep parts of Him.

That night I saw that having taken small steps toward receiving more of Him wasn't satisfying my hunger; it was creating more of it.

The paint still smelled fresh in our master bedroom when I saw her. Nate and I were beginning to feel the emptiness of our big house that could hold a family. God was no longer creating space only on the inside. We were being readied for both pain and joy too great to hold ahead of time.

I sat on my bed one morning in prayer — about what, I'm not sure. Then it came over me. He came over me. His Spirit overshadowed me. I saw her in my mind's eye, this little brown-skinned, almond-eyed girl, crawling across my comforter.

No words were spoken out loud, but my spirit received that she would be my daughter. For a moment, His presence allowed the vision for adoption that Nate and I'd had at Chinquapin to become personal.

Just as surely as I knew she was — would be — my daughter, I knew she was African. My understanding expanded without a single word. I tasted the Spirit of wisdom and revelation, so other, so intimate.

One moment I carried expectations of my life and what it might look like, and then the next, I received an entirely new reality.

God comes in the mundane and shifts us, slightly and subtly. Suddenly and slowly, it is following Him in the unseen that feels most normal.

I was left wondering what to do with this encounter. I recounted it to Nate matter-of-factly, as if I were telling him what I ate for lunch. He didn't protest. He received, as I had.

But what next?

Something told me this vision was not for now, but my desire to be obedient to the veritable handwritten note I'd received from Him sent me searching.

Was there anywhere to adopt in Africa?

At the time, the answer was no. I contacted a ministry we'd followed out of Mozambique, and their response wasn't hopeful — live in-country for three years and you could possibly be approved. A distant friend had adopted a small child from Kenya, but when I contacted their social worker, my suspicions were accurate. This was an isolated adoption that wouldn't likely see a second.

So I filed it away, without discouragement. We would have our biological lot and then, one day, would pursue this little beauty my mind's eye had seen as I prayed.

For Your Continued Pursuit

John 13:34–35 | 1 John 4:7–10 | John 15:9, 12 | 1 Thessalonians 3:12 | Psalm 139:15 | Song of Solomon 1:5 | Ephesians 3:20 | Psalm 139:17–18 | James 1:2–4 | Romans 8:18 | 2 Corinthians 4:8–10 | 1 Peter 4:12–13 | Isaiah 64:4

six

WHISPERS IN THE DARK

"You are my private garden, my treasure, my bride."

She wore the glow I wanted, the glow I'd practiced. I'd never noticed it until it had become something that eluded me, but as months of childlessness stretched behind me—and ahead—I wanted what I couldn't have.

After all, something about pregnancy ignites confidence in a woman. I know it because I've window-shopped that look for some time now. I could see it in my friend, who had just made her happy announcement. She'd been vetted and got a yes. Chosen to conceive, worthy to carry the life of another within. *Blessed.*

As usual, my selfishness felt unfettered as I struggled to celebrate the gain of another while staring deeply into my own loss. Most days, I could approach my pain, measured, but when the eruption of holiness in another's womb reminded me of my not-yet, I buckled.

"I know how you must feel," she said. "When we didn't get pregnant that first month, I got really nervous that something was wrong."

I went under, to that murky place where no human can retrieve me.

Her sentiment was beautiful. She was reaching across the

chasm between her new reality and the cliff to which I'd been relegated. She leaned. She tried.

But that was just it—she had to *try* to understand. The fact that her experience made it impossible for her to connect with me made her healing words wounding. I had entered into a land where very few could know, intimately, the pain of time bearing down on me.

Her words were the least of the misunderstandings I'd experienced in the years that my womb remained empty and the emotional layers of my life peeled like old paint. It was clear that she *wanted* to enter my story. She'd attempted to reach me, something beyond so many others who came before and after her, but my story itself made me unreachable.

One month? What I wouldn't have given to know the walls of this purgatory for only one month. Instead I'd studied those walls for years, known their cracks, felt their coldness.

I thought back to the first month. What did that feel like? Was I nervous, afraid? Did I have any anxiety about the pregnancy tests to come? No, after one month I was still vibrant with expectancy. In fact, I looked back on that time as my glory days. I didn't know then that I'd log years in this waiting room. I didn't know then that the women alongside me, all waiting their turn to bear glory, would have their numbers called while I waited still.

Over time, some people entered my waiting room with kid gloves, and others barged in, uninvited, providing commentary on those parts of me that were weakest. Each time as they came and went, I moved from *Do they even know what it's like to have this kind of pain?* to *Do they even really know me?* and then *Does anyone even know me?*

The world calls it loneliness. At the time I had trouble labeling it anything other than pain. It just hurt.

But God allowed it. Maybe even invited it.

Could it be these *are my glory days?*

College had witnessed Nate's first growth spurt. By what can be attributed only to the hand of God, Nate landed himself amid a group of boys (ready to be men) who had an early understanding that no part of knowing God is passive. They had a zest for life and for Him and for a life in Him.

They wrestled in the basement of a college-house-made-into-bullpen, pushed the furniture back and let the floor absorb their sweat as they sought to strong-arm one another. The walls heard late-night conversations about God and impact and a life lived alive. They played, hard, and loved Him and one another, hard.

Though I came into the picture after the caps and gowns had been boxed, I witnessed their dreams take wing in their twenties. By that point, many of them wore rings of allegiance to women who gave them not only permission to pursue that flight of life in God but access to it.

These men and their wives followed God to the run-down parts of a Virginia city and planted a stake there that said, *He loves in unexpected ways.* They bought houses for pennies and relinquished their Wall Street opportunities for back-alley living. They loved those whom many deemed to be unlovable. They reached the unreached with a life, not just a message. They lived the Sermon on the Mount. They did it. They poured their lives into a cup of cold water for the poor.

During those years of transition and sacrifice for them, Nate and I simply watched.

I wrestled with guilt over not joining this band of brothers on their venture. For so long, I had understood life as impact for God's kingdom. But as Nate and I struggled in the shadows of our fledgling marriage, I realized I had little to give. I couldn't force my way into another's story the way I had so readily in years past. We had no cup of cold water to offer and weren't quite sure we knew how to drink ourselves.

I had no choice but to survive, and survival, for me, meant finding this God I'd said yes to on that snowy night in November so many years before. I wet my journal with tears and unstuck the pages of my Bible. I talked to Him. A lot. I made Scripture my prayer and paced the first floor of my house in darkened mornings and after the sun went down, asking to see the face of God. I sought my first love.

I formed vague responses in conversations with old friends who asked how we were doing. They once knew me as the driven one who'd do anything for the kingdom. I wasn't that girl anymore, but I didn't know who I was now. I just was beginning to know Him.

I slumped in my chair when others talked about the vision they had for reaching their communities for God. I didn't know how to walk out my front door with confidence. I was being stripped of all I knew, whittled down to just this one thing: Him.

Those first few years of marriage, I thought that this would be my new spiritual life: I would forever be stripped of any outward ability to make a dent in the world, but I would know, secretly, that I moved God's heart. I was growing to understand that this season that felt stalled was not one for me to despise. It was one that He not only loved but orchestrated. He liked me when no one was looking. He enjoyed my private devotion.

He was *jealous*. For *me*.

But just when I'd settled in to living in that small space I had carved, He spoke words of change.

Out of this deep crying-out to God, a time that had more to do with impacting God's heart than impacting the world, came the call.

Adopt.

Several more years into our marriage and a few years into the reality of a barren womb, God reignited the same notion He had placed in our heads that first night at Chinquapin.

I didn't know then that one child would lead to two, would lead to four (and possibly to more). As with any calling, we dip our toes in the water of yes and hope to God that this is the biggest yes we'll have to utter, the biggest move our hearts will have to make with such trust, only to find ourselves submerged, years later.

God was bringing a glory out of this barrenness and a greater hunger for Him out of our longing. This new desire for an old concept—impact—came not from pressing or forcing, as we once had, but from receiving. He whispered in the dark, when no one else was looking. And we were there, hidden, to hear Him.

It was a bitter cold Sunday in December when my heart wore the weather.

At the time, we were attending a church teeming with prolific twentysomethings. Most all the women my age (or younger) were pregnant, nursing, or carrying their six-month-olds strapped to their chests in a tight wrap.

They came on Sundays, in droves, it felt, to be reminded of a faithful God, but I entered those doors each week with the stinging sense that my request of that same faithful God hadn't yet received a response. They were my reminders.

This particular Sunday, Nate was out of town. I was doing announcements for church, so I couldn't pull the covers up over my head and forfeit my weekly encounter with envy.

This, however, was the day that produced a forever change in perspective. As we sang the worship songs, I couldn't keep the question mark over my life from manifesting itself as pain. Tears slipped out from underneath the eyelids I'd clamped shut. I didn't want to let anyone into this place. Being among those blessed only made me feel even more cursed.

Our adoption process had recently hit a paperwork road-block, one of several over the past months and years. The end seemed farther away than when we'd first started. It all felt like playing house to me—these discussions and preparations for our adoption. *You're just a little girl with a big imagination*, the enemy in my thoughts teased me. The road to family seemed impassable at every junction, and the words of these worship songs felt void next to my reality.

Like most pain that we withhold from God's touch, my paper pregnancy (apparently now also barren) had fostered a fermentation within my heart. My hurt was expanding beyond "just" the issues of childbearing and was touching the broader vision for my life. I was looking at life through the lens of being overlooked by God.

I kept my eyes closed to keep the others around me from view—those whom, I naively assumed, could more easily proclaim the truths of God in song because they had what I wanted.

Then I saw a vision on the back of my eyelids: the word *family* scribbled across a piece of paper. The paper had a nail through its center, affixing it to a cross. The Lord whispered inside my spirit as I saw it: *If you never have a family, will you still love Me?*

I walked out of church that day, hardened. Had it really come to this? The very idea that what I most feared — becoming stamped with the word *barren* — was now not only a possibility but a suggestion ... and from God?

I had no answer to God's question. I, the one who had once youthfully boasted of my willingness to be martyred for the sake of Jesus, couldn't say yes to God when He asked me for allegiance in the face of His no.

The crazy thing about all of this is that I never really wanted to be a mom.

I wasn't the little girl who played house and dreamed about changing diapers and dressed myself up as mommy. In my late teens and early twenties, I didn't even want to get married. Marriage and children were far from desirable to my driven heart. I saw them as obstacles to a devoted life, not as ways to get there.

When God broke in and gave me the desire to have children, I assumed that His initiative would also mean a speedy follow-through. He pricked our hearts for adoption that night at Chinquapin, and then shortly thereafter He nudged me toward the desire for biological children that I knew was other, of Him. This was well before I even deemed myself ready. He initiated the desire.

So in my mind, God's question during that encounter in

church had less to do with the content—having a family—and more to do with His nature. Why would He put this desire deep within my core only to ask me to relinquish it? Why invite me to travel a road with a dead end?

It took me three days to respond.

I knew the right answer, but I couldn't speak it.

Instead, I spent hours picturing a life like the one God was asking me to consider, void of family but full of Him. Could I love a God who might take away the very desire He put in me? Could I trust the leadership of a Man when the mystery He offered wasn't wondrous but perplexing? Could I further engage with the very One on whose watch I was wounded?

Somehow, out of this darkness, which seemed so bleak, came a response that I didn't expect. It was so unlike me that I knew I was being overshadowed. The Holy Spirit erected a resolve in my soul that my flesh could not have produced.

Yes!

I was made for this yes, and the God whose Spirit meshed with mine inside of me produced it.

The question and His answer, from within me, changed everything.

Yes, I could love Him. Yes, I could trust His leadership. Yes, I could even find delight and joy and contentment living from the underside of mystery—perplexity.

Yes, there was a dance to be danced in this valley.

Instead of letting all that I lacked consume me, I was being made ready to delve into unknown frontiers of Him. His call, here, was louder than the life for which I'd begun to fantasize.

The same God-man looked different than He had to me even one week before. He was my opportunity, not my dead end.

I suddenly wanted Him more than His promises.

Was it possible to have a retroactive perspective? If so, I did. Years of vacancy now felt like opulence.

Like one, lame, who'd just been healed to walk, I kept trying out my legs. I pictured the end as He suggested it. Did it hurt? Could I walk there? A life without the dream He'd given me still left me full of questions, but something was settled on the inside that hadn't been before.

I wanted Him.

Whether He came and lifted my circumstances, or He just came.

It could be good enough. Better than good enough.

This God-man nudged me out across my imagined fears and unveiled Himself.

And I? I began the ascent from rejected to chosen. Even when my circumstances were unbending, God was good to me.

Within minutes of arriving at the waiting area where my siblings and my mom had spent their evening, my lighthearted approach to a day's travel turned sour. Dreadfully sour.

Nate and I rounded the corner with smiles on our faces, ready to receive the bunch that had been—just hours earlier—sending us hopeful updates. We found a very different scene than we anticipated.

The surgeon offered me a sympathetic look when my mom introduced us, as if I somehow could have already known the news she had just delivered. My brother was stifling tears on the head of his soon-to-be bride, her consoling arms wrapped around his waist. My sister's shock was buffered only by the three fingers she had wrapped around my mom's hand, needing the reminder of hope that human touch offers.

"It's not good," said my brother. There was no time to ease into the reality that they'd had a few minutes to absorb.

My mom hugged me tight to her chest, needing to comfort her little girl, needing the comfort of an adult pulse while her husband's faltered. The surgeon inconspicuously left her post. Her job was done.

As the shock wore off, we dissected the meaning behind her piercing words. Words like *brain cancer* and *rapid growth* and *stage four* and *twelve to eighteen months left* were my acclimation to what I'd believed up until that point was easily resolvable.

My daddy was dying.

The night that followed still is, to date, the worst night of my life. My body went into a fit that my mind and heart could not get a grip on. As my siblings gathered their belongings and ushered my mom to another sterile waiting room in the hospital, I collapsed.

My body melted under the weight of the message and its implications. I folded myself up on the floor and wept. Cold hard tile became a bed for my tears. Limp, already broken, I thought I was on the road to recovery, but this blow was a major setback. My body couldn't bear up under the grief I'd been carrying.

Just days earlier I had scrawled my newly inherited perspective on the pages of my journal. I was rounding the corner to the new year in every way. Promise had surfaced in my life. We'd had small circumstantial changes that had translated into fragile hope. But hope was hope. There were no gradations. I hadn't had this sort of quickening of spirit in years.

Not only was my spirit changing, our adoption process had picked up speed. We were number one on the waitlist to receive news of the ones who would soon be ours. Signs of new life were also surfacing in our marriage. Detox had run its course and health was springing up.

Morning had broken.

For a few days, at least.

When I heard that my dad's overnight stay had turned into a several-night stay and that the doctors were quickly eliminating the diagnoses that would have been easily treatable, I wrapped my fingers tighter around hope. *This will be another instance of seeing God's goodness*, I thought with the buoyancy of my new perspective.

But how quickly we let ourselves feel cursed again.

That night in the hospital, my age-old fear surfaced again like a stain. "Forever" beliefs dissipated into familiar thoughts: *Of course. This is just how my life goes. Why should I expect it to be different? If I want something, it will always elude me.*

With my family, I curled up on dated pieces of waiting-room furniture. Christmas music rang through the speakers overhead, a postmidnight airing of a choir performance. Darkness slid its veil over my heart, but I didn't sleep.

Life was running red, the colors of all my circumstances blending into one river on which I couldn't stay afloat.

"Tonight is critical," said the surgeon, reentering our growing grief. This time she was dressed in a silver silk Christmas outfit, getting ready to leave the hospital for a holiday party. Standing in the glare of the hallway's fluorescent lights, she said, "You need to brace yourself for the fact that he may not make it through the night."

Winter's warmth of fire and friends beckoned her while we stared grimly into the face of death. This was her job. This was our lives. And even I, an advocate of God's healing touch, was left without words. What does faith look like in the face of expert opinion? Her word against His?

She left for her gathering, and we each cried silent tears to ourselves, knowing that a word spoken out loud might turn what we were hoping was myth into reality.

The year I first met God as Father was the year my father died.

Ten months after his diagnosis, we stood at his gravesite. My fervent prayers for healing were buried in the Father. Buried with my father.

Only God knew those late-night tears I cried deep into the pillow of my parents' basement bedroom. I wept beneath the floor my dad had padded across night after night as he searched for answers in the haze that had become his brain. I was searching for answers in the haze that had become my life.

My mother, his best friend, took the night watch as his world got smaller and his cancer cells grew. Nate and I spent weeks no longer as guests in their home, wanting to lift any load we could. God had sent us there under the guise of offering help, but really I was there to receive.

Dad and I played cards, watched movies, and talked about God while his brain was still active. We sat in the comfortable silence of companionship when he got lost in the vacancy of his mind, overgrown with malignancy.

All the while, I prayed two prayers: *Father, heal him* and *Father, let me know You.*

The first prayer came reluctantly but passionately in that hospital waiting room on December 22. The second was familiar, still growing as I grew.

I knew *of* the Father-love, but it was unfamiliar to me.

My experience with my own dad didn't fit with the experience of friends who had absent or cruel dads. I understood how they struggled to move beyond acquaintanceship with God, but I was an anomaly. I had a loving earthly father and couldn't conceptualize the love of God the Father.

My dad gave the best of himself to me and to my siblings. He abandoned what he knew from his own father and chose to be a patriarch who demonstrated his love to his children. My daddy's arms were safe. I was alive under my father's gaze.

Perplexed that even in light of my own father's expressed love, I couldn't get my arms around God's love, I continued to pray. Prayers that filled pages soon filled journals and then shelves.

I knew God as a powerful Leader. I saw signs of Him as Shepherd, carefully guiding my weak heart. I grew to love Him as Savior; I believed in sin's sting being diminished at the foot of that wooden cross. Pain brought the face of God as Sanctifier. Even Deliverer.

But Father?

God was still a "lesson" to me—a practice or a discipline, even a habit—but I didn't know how to wrap my arms around the idea of calling Him Daddy.

Then my dad died.

God's response to my first prayer was "not yet," and my dad slipped through my fingers. Simultaneously, God's response to my second: a blossoming.

A shift began inside of me just after my father died that was almost unquantifiable. I'd come across friends and authors over the years who'd spoken about the Father-love of God. It was something I wanted, something that still felt elusive to me. I'd asked. I'd prayed. I'd journaled. *I want to know You, as Father.*

I'd reached with the sort of reaching that comes from one who knows her missing piece is critical.

Now God came. My heart mourned the loss of my daddy in the same month that it received the understanding of God as a tender Father. To me.

His Fathering hand would hold me in the days ahead.

For Your Continued Pursuit

Romans 8:18 | Matthew 10:42 | Hebrews 4:12 | 1 Chronicles 15:11 | Psalm 119:10 | Revelation 2:4 | Exodus 20:4–5 | 2 Samuel 22:29 | Psalm 23:4 | Psalm 23:1 | Luke 9:23–25 | Psalm 119:68 | Psalm 68:5 | Matthew 23:9 | Romans 8:15 | Isaiah 64:8 | John 14:6, 9 | Ephesians 3:14–15 | 1 John 3:1

seven

THE REAL MIRACLE

"And I will look up."

It came as a series of text messages, before texting was commonplace. I was buried deep in my Bible, and God was singling out my husband.

First, Nate alerted me that "the business financials are bad."

At the time, our dark season of waiting for children was lingering longer than we'd anticipated. We'd had infusions of hope, but circumstances were unreliable. One day we'd see movement with our adoption that made us ready to declare a new day, and then the next day came another delay. Just as with my father's diagnosis and death, circumstances were like sand in our hands.

The day before Nate's text, I'd thought, *Now we've hit bottom. It can't get worse than this.*

So when the text came, I didn't brace myself. *It can't be that bad,* I thought.

I was sitting before God. This place had become familiar. It was steady. I could shut the door to the unpredictable around me and seek out this One who, though also not predictable, was consistently available to give me a framework for all this external mess. I'd come to know Him as friend, available for me here, in times just like this.

For many years pain caused me to shut down. I had ready

89

access to activity, and this activity became my diversion when I didn't know what to do with an ache that surfaced in front of me. He was distant, then, and I was on the move.

But one or two instances of sitting, not running, when life hurt, introduced me to a new way. Sitting before Him when our adoption stalled and asking the questions that a little girl asks her daddy when life isn't what she expected made it all the more easy to go there again when another month passed and my womb was empty. When my dad died, I found that place again.

I could talk to God. More than talk, even, I could expect an exchange in which I came, barren, and He responded with something so other that the instance itself was overshadowed by what He was offering me. It was as if I could feel the rise and fall of His chest simply by pausing enough to rest on it.

God was revealing this kind of availability to me in both the big aches and the everyday small ones.

The nearness of God in this new way was alluring enough that I'd made a habit of it, such that when more news came, I *wanted* back in that place with Him.

The second text, and then the third, revealed the details. This was worse than we'd thought.

Within minutes, I went from imagining a lesser monthly income to preparing for no monthly income to wondering if this business would tank in a matter of days.

Nate, green to running his own business, had made a simple bookkeeping mistake in how he categorized his funds. That error hid an accruing debt from plain sight, for months. Then, one day, he stumbled upon the mountain of red on which his business had been built.

He was in tens of thousands of dollars of debt. *We*, as business owners who made a principle of avoiding debt, were now in tens of thousands of dollars of debt.

We met for lunch after this revelation, he stunned and I unnaturally steady. God had been reconfiguring me, early, before I had language for what would transpire here.

"We'll dance on this," I said. "This isn't our darkest hour but our best." I spoke words I'd only just begun to believe for myself and was surprised to hear myself say them. It was as if speaking them reinforced my belief in them.

Nate had wrapped his arms around me during my unraveling for years, and now it was my turn to hold him during his. It was my turn to remind him we were blessed, not cursed.

Yes, God was good ... to us.

With circumstances spiraling and hearts still tangled in perplexity, we were seeing His goodness. This—all this mess— was fodder for discovering His love anew.

Every single dark day was an invitation.

For days and weeks this accounting error reverberated through Nate's business and into our home. The money we'd saved to cover a portion of our adoption expenses, and a little cushion to fall back on was the money we'd now have to live on. We kept a keen eye on what we thought might be yet another thing to go in this season of stripping: his fairly new marketing and consulting business.

These were new days of want.

And all this unfolded just months after I had a strong nudge from the Lord not to share the financial needs of our adoption with anyone beyond a few close friends.

We appeared as if we had no need, and now we didn't feel

released to voice the other story happening behind our closed doors.

This was my opportunity to live a new reality. To stare, every day, into another layer of this unpredictable pain and delay and believe a different truth. Survival required a new kind of seeing.

But this loss leveled Nate. Every struggle over the years touched each of us differently. This one hit him hard. *How did I get us here?* was the question of his every moment. This "mistake" indoctrinated him in shame. Clarity had a hard time breaking through.

But God had allowed this error—and all of Nate's internal wrestling that surfaced as a result—in response to our hunger. We wanted the deep parts of us to find the deep parts of Him, and both hunger and its companion, pain, have a way of exposing us to His touch.

He had something for us, here.

I had a lot of ideas about God that weren't actually God's ideas about God. When our lives initially got stretched through our marital pain, the picture I had of Him couldn't stand beside the struggles we were facing. My prayers felt rote because of how I saw the One to whom I was praying.

Then with each successive layer of circumstantial pain, new false ideas of God that we'd carried were unearthed. The pain of infertility, the adoption delays, my father's death, and now this business setback all revealed ways in which I saw God that didn't line up with what His Word said about Him.

I needed a shift, foundationally, in order to grow up and out of these skewed ideas.

My first step in inhaling adoration was inviting that language into my everyday ache.

Adoration.

I started with one word, or one phrase from His Word. Some days, it was an aspect of God's character that resonated with a particular need. If I was caught in a mind trap, condemning myself for failing in some area, this was my time to hold His Word up against the "truth" I'd contrived. So that's where I started. I read from the Psalms, "Your faithfulness reaches to the clouds." I prayed, *God, You are faithful. You are faithful when I am fearful. I can count on You. You will not leave me when You see my failure.*

In that way, the irritant of the day became the conversation God and I carried on throughout it. I scribbled notes in my Moleskine journal, propped next to my Bible near my kitchen sink, stained by carrot peels and smelling of onions. I invited His Word into my head, the place most parched for His reality.

If I didn't have a specific circumstance stirring me toward a characteristic of God, I searched the Psalms. Line upon line, this book showed the chasm in my understanding. Line upon line, this book brought me back to adoration as a way to bridge the chasm between my perceptions and God's truth. Day after day, I felt the relief of holding my toxic thoughts up to His beauty.

I saw more clearly the disconnection between who I said God is and who I believed Him to be. I saw that pain wasn't a result of my circumstances; pain was a result of my detachment from the Father. Circumstances were merely unearthing my view of life.

It was adoration—practicing, trying it out, seeing what it looked like in my life—that led me to this new perspective on God. It led me to a Father who longs not merely to be served but also to be known. Who longs for us, His creation, to know the cadence of His heartbeat.

I pressed pause on my day to say His Word back to Him. I aligned my haphazard thought life with the Truth that changes. I started the habit of telling Him who He is, using His Word. And I let His Word reframe my experience.

As I utter those strong words about Him with my weak voice, words I can barely believe when they leave my mouth, something inside of me shifts.

I begin to know Him not through my own interpretation but through His.

Adoration is exploration. The Father loves to be explored.

We underestimate the power that our knowing Him has in moving His heart. We underestimate the power that our moving His heart has on our lives.

Fear loses oxygen when every moment suspends itself under the purpose of bringing Him glory, of knowing His name and His nature.

Sometimes, instead of leading us up and out of those very fears, big and small, He lets us live them.

He gives us over to them.

Because it's in this giving over to our fears that we find the perfect love that frees us from them. Forever.

The weeks and months after we found ourselves in this financial swamp, we expected to live with it sucking us deeper down. Nate braced himself, almost daily, for the blows he figured he deserved for his business mistake. He lived in a self-constructed purgatory.

As had been true through most of our marriage, we rode

the teeter-totter. This time, he was down and I was up. So many times it had been the reverse. But in those months, the me who had been so inclined toward fear knew peace. And so we each walked in new places, neither better nor worse than the other. Both creatively spun by God.

Month after month we whittled down our little adoption nest egg until our bank balances ran close to zero. New bills rolled in and we watched their deadlines vigilantly, this time without a plan for how to cover our adoption.

What also began to grow in this low season were the testimonies. Our stories of His abundance. The check that came, unsolicited, to cover a few months' expenses. The bills that, somehow, got paid, month after month. The business that crept its way toward being out of the hole.

God was working every angle to change our knowledge about who He is. We realized that our lives aren't, in fact, a series of rewards for doing things "right." They are strung-together surprises that continue to speak more of who He is than who we aren't.

We wondered to each other, whispering, *What if all of life, all of our understanding of God, starts—first—with Him?*

Circumstances still would have failed us had we simply decided our lives were about "really good faith stories." Like a child growing up on sweets, our craving for the gifts from His hand would have only grown. Each new testimony would be forgotten in light of the next breakthrough we desired.

But when God helped us see circumstances as the catalyst to a new understanding of Him, they became the testimony of Jesus in our lives. *Look! Not at what is happening to us but at what that says about God.*

There we were, gulping mercy, as God doled out events that

allowed us to look at Him anew. Hard and challenging though they were, they forged a new perspective. Each one came from Him to us with an opportunity to shape our praise back to Him.

And then the call: "I'd like you to tear up the promissory note," he said on the other end of the line, not quite a year after we plummeted into that hole of debt.

Can tens of thousands of dollars really be forgiven, just like that?

We spent the night in shock, though the shock itself should have been our shock. Our God had been telling us through His Word's unfolding that this is who He is.

The mistake for which Nate thought he'd spend a lifetime making penance shifted into his greatest testimony during the course of one conversation, this one man's conversation with God. A year before, he'd offered Nate a better rate than what the bank could offer him to handle this unexpected debt. Little did we know that this generous extension would move from loan to gift.

The sprinkling of God-surprises had certainly increased during our season of want. We lived the demonstration of His grace, undeserved yet rich in His outpouring as we discovered our hearts' debts to be forgiven. And now this. The Father went to great lengths to reorient our understanding of Him.

Trust, which had already weaved itself into our understanding because of what His Word said about Him, now had a part in our story. That loan note, torn into pieces, was a seal over what God had already been doing in us.

We didn't need our own miracle to believe that God can

perform miracles. His Word already speaks this truth. We needed His perspective, sown into our inner understanding of Him, to be able not just to witness but to receive the real miracle He was working.

Again, it was looking at Him, long and rightly, that was performing miracles.

Adoration makes walking with God more than just reacting to a series of externals. Adoration calls the circumstances, no matter how high or low, into proper submission in our hearts. Adoration roots us in a reality that no amount of pain and no amount of blessing can shake.

Adoration steadies us. It repatterns our thinking. It centers our lives around a God-man instead of forever trying to make sense of the God-man through the lenses of our circumstances.

Adoration aligns us under Him. This is the place where life is found.

One day, we woke up knowing we had tens of thousands of dollars of debt behind our name without a forgiveness plan. It had been there for nearly a year. The next morning, that debt was all gone.

And it wasn't through our ingenuity or business acumen.

But the beauty of it all was that our perspective on Him was not altered. It was enhanced.

Circumstances didn't shape us.

He did, ahead of time.

Thus the pain of life, against God's Word and whispers, comes to look like opportunity. Each blow has a treasure of Him, hidden deep, made for our searching out.

What our flesh resisted, our souls now craved: an expansion of our inner lives as our outer lives were being compressed.

When our season of financial debt ended, the circumstantial relief was only an afterthought.

The real miracle had been happening all along.

For Your Continued Pursuit

2 Corinthians 4:18 | Psalm 42:7 | Proverbs 16:9 | Psalm 34:19 | Isaiah 55:8–9 | 2 Timothy 3:16–17 | Psalm 36:5–6 | Isaiah 28:10 | Psalm 119:9 | Psalm 100:2–5 | Jeremiah 9:23–24 | 2 Corinthians 4:6 | 1 John 4:18 | Psalm 56:4 | Psalm 119:14–16 | Psalm 86:5 | 1 Peter 2:2 | Psalm 1:2

eight

THE PLACE
WHERE ASKING BEGINS

"Hope that is seen is not hope."

Nate and I drove an hour beyond our exit, at midnight, just to savor the sweet presence of God that was in our car. This night was different. New.

Just a few days previous, I had prayed a simple prayer. *God, give me Your eyes for the one You have called me to. Let me see Nate how You see him.* Old conflicts had resurfaced, and I was relating to Nate in a way that felt stale. Not only were my words painful to him, but my heart was distant. I had developed a habit of fixing my eyes on what Nate was not, instead of seeing the strength of God inside of him.

I circled back to these patterns of thinking just as I circled back to the stale thoughts of what *I* was not. It was an old habit.

Each time I revisited this way of thinking and seeing, I discovered new layers of false understandings of God. God's love, to me, still stopped short when we fell short. He was a loving Father—to a point—but when I failed *consistently*, God seemed to me to be a middle-age man, tired of my failure, exasperated by what I wasn't, and too stretched to extend grace.

So I, then, took on that stance toward Nate. I was tired of his failure. I homed in on what he wasn't. I was tired of his humanity. I was too tired to extend the kind of grace that changes a person, the kind of grace that sees their effort and loves them for their untiring attempts to get back up and walk toward God.

What led me to pray this prayer, days before, was that I'd seen that Nate was not impervious to my growing scrutiny. I'd watched this man whose arms had been strong enough to hold me during my most tangled moments, many of which directed anger at him, now *feeling* the weight of my limited perspective on him. But I didn't know what to do with that. I'd wounded him not only with the words I'd said but with the affirmation I'd withheld in an effort to prod him toward change. Now I didn't know how to cover those wounds.

I was at a loss to love Nate, unnaturally, the way God had loved me, unnaturally, through Nate. I needed a shift in how I saw him that my flesh couldn't produce.

The tail end of that nine-hour drive back from my childhood hometown was when God chose to give that shift. That night, God erected a memorial in our marriage that we still point to today.

I began to speak words I couldn't feel until they were said, out loud. I affirmed. I called forth who Nate is, the Nate whom no one but God and I had seen. It was this night that Nate let me into the parts of him that were weak and insecure so that I might, this time, be the hand that held those wounds. This was the night I administered a love I'd only just begun to know.

God gave me His words and His feelings toward Nate, and I spoke with a love that looks not just past failure but through it, to call forth the beauty underneath. I didn't just affirm; I partnered with the Father to heal.

God's words through me that night reached through the

exterior Nate had built around himself, protecting the parts of him that feared he would never be the man I needed, or the man he wanted to be. I cradled parts of him he'd never before exposed to me. Somehow God helped me reach up into His heart and speak what I saw and felt there.

As I spoke the words, my mind raced with thoughts. *Is this really how God sees a heart? Can God change my perspective in an instant?* But the power of the words I released lifted my eyes to the God who delivered them. God's Father-love came in, when I spoke it out. I learned it as I said it. Delight and life from a tongue can change a soul.

God was renaming us, each through the other.

When we'd first moved from Chinquapin into our new home, I had a moment, followed by a few other moments, when God broke in. It wasn't mystical. In fact, it felt very natural. God spoke to me not audibly but as a resounding sense in my spirit. As far as I could tell, He said to me, *You will conceive a child this September.*

Now, while I believe in the voice of God speaking today, I am also wary of what I know even more intimately — my flesh. I can hear things I want to hear, and my imagination, at times, might be just as clear as what I perceive to be the voice of God. So I asked Him for confirmation. *Lord, if this is You, confirm it — not once but twice.*

The details of His confirmation were enough for me to believe, with as much of my being as I was capable, that Nate and I would be parents the next summer, nine months following September of 2005. I thought God gracious to prepare me, one who might benefit from having more than the typically allotted time to carry a baby.

At that time, we had no idea the fertility challenges awaiting us. Like most young wives, I assumed that "trying" to have children means conceiving children.

So leading up to that September, I lived confident that I would be pregnant soon. I didn't waver in my expectation. I had no reason to. I had heard from God other times, but never this clearly. Never did a sense I had *or* a nudge from Him carry the grace that this message did to spur on my prayers. I wound up thanking God for what He was about to do more than even asking Him to do it.

This was going to happen.

In early October, I realized that the expectation I'd held with such confidence was false. There was no baby in my womb. The disappointment that flooded me had less to do with Him and more to do with me. I didn't doubt God, but I questioned my ability to hear. Was it time to question my sanity? God wasn't unfaithful; I just couldn't hear Him.

All my life I had set up camp on the side of caution, leery of anyone who "heard" from God. Interpretation was dangerous, and I was now living the fulfillment of that very danger. I'd spent three months wasting time planning on a vaporlike outcome, all based on a sense I felt I was given that something was coming.

Little did I know that one month of disappointment was a precursor to nearly a decade of tasting the same bitter flavor. It wasn't only one September that I didn't conceive. It was many Septembers, Octobers, and Novembers in the years ahead. Every question I had about what I'd believed God had promised fit into a backpack I wore into every interaction I had with Him, like the memory of a marital betrayal. *Remember this?*

Four years passed before I gained any insight into that particular exchange with God.

In March of 2009, we received our referral for two children from Ethiopia after an arduous year and a half in the hamster wheel of adoption. A pint-sized girl and her little brother. I found myself giddy at times, unable to sleep, dreaming about holding these two for whom we'd waited for so long.

Months later, we prepared to get them. To cross the expanse of one segment of our waiting in the form of the Atlantic Ocean. Africa held a fulfillment—them for us, and us for them.

Weeks before we left, our case was heard in Ethiopia. Just after we passed court, we received our little girl's birth date.

September 2005.

When a mother on one continent gave birth to a child, that same child was conceived for another mother, halfway around the world. One little girl's birth was this adoptive mom's conception. The day she was begotten on this earth, she was destined to be mine.

Months before our referral, I asked the Lord to confirm that these two children were ours.

He knew before I asked and gave me confirmation. Four years earlier. As if to say, *Prepare. Wait. It will be a long gestation, but you will give birth. Your conception lies in another mother's birth.*

September no longer held a sting for me. It brought new life.

The darkness of waiting, and many of its questions, had a new name. It was no longer a tomb, but a holding place for resurrection.

My wilderness gave way to Eden.

And yet.

My hand gripped the edge of the bathroom sink as I once again scrutinized the pregnancy test. Was there (maybe?) a faint line I was missing in this light?

I didn't count the number of tests I'd taken. There were no line items in our monthly budget for check, check, and double check. But maybe there should have been. Even a negative result is an indicator that hope is still alive. Every time I took a test, I believed, again, that this barrenness might end.

I ran my fingers across my midriff, the womb that had not yet known child, my body absent of the stretch marks so many women wish they didn't have.

Even with two children in my home with whom I could not be more in love, I felt the ache of my body, broken. My barrenness remained a question mark over my life, even now that I was a mother.

How is it that adoption didn't completely fill my mommy void? I was beginning to conclude that that void wasn't really a mommy void at all. I wasn't longing to have my skin stretch to hold another. I rarely felt the ache to have a child who looked like Nate and me. I hadn't spent my young adult days dreaming about pregnancy. My continued grief, my longing, was not a sign of dissatisfaction with the children God had given me. I loved them as my own flesh.

I struggled, instead, with knowing that God *could* heal me, but He hadn't.

It seemed like ages ago that I had sat in the doctor's sterile office, which sought to be promising with its photographs of newborn babies pressed against smiling mommies whose bodies, unlike mine, were complete. His bookshelves held catchy titles that said the opposite of his words. Instead of discussing *The Fastest Way to Conceive*, he said, "You're an unusual case. Your body is hardwired with a condition that many women are able to change through diet and nutrition. Though this isn't impossible, it won't be easy for you."

Despite his words, I left the office full of expectation that God would trump this diagnosis. "What may take some people one year could very well take you six," said this doctor. But when six years passed and I had watched a number of friends with this very condition conceive their first child and then their second and, some, their third, I remembered his words.

I had become that unusual case.

Standing at the bathroom sink, the suggested two-minute wait turned into four minutes, five, seven, and I dropped the plastic eight ball of a test into the trash can. I curled up on my bed and tried to think of something else, anything other than absorbing the impact of another month's delay.

I thought about those who had watched me persist in prayer, against all odds. *What will they say about You, Father?*

But what I really meant to say to God was, *What does* my heart *say about You, Daddy?*

Another minute passed and I dragged the test out of the trash can.

Maybe, just maybe.

Nope.

At least the day before, I'd basked in hope. I'd made plans. I'd told the story in my head a hundred times. Expectant mother, expectant of God. He came through. *I told you so*, I said to those voices telling me that I was wasting time begging His ear when I could have rested in His sovereignty.

But it wasn't to be this time. Not yet.

Oh, Father, how long?

The props that had comforted me when a test was negative—the run for a chai, the venting session with a girlfriend, the media escape—would not be enough that day. I knew they never had been.

Fetuslike on my bed, I had only moments before little African feet would scamper across the floor and find me as their jungle gym. But He held time for me as holy pain created a crack within. This moment had a work to do, and God multiplied what little time I had to receive it.

I knew that my womb wasn't the only thing barren. My inability to respond with trust, to lean, to rest peacefully in what God *could* do, but *hadn't* done, exposed me. My instant response to that moment over my bathroom sink, to many moments like it, was far from eyes-on-Him. Instead of saying, *Show me Yourself as Healer,* I asked, *Why haven't You healed me?* Instead of saying, *Show me the Daddy side of You,* I asked, *Why aren't You Daddy to me?* Instead of saying, *Show me Yourself as Comforter of those in pain,* I asked, *Why all the pain?*

My questions revealed my resistance to the vulnerability God loves. If I'd let it, weakness would continue to produce a need in me that would draw me nearer to Him.

I had surely grown since that first negative pregnancy test, but there was still much more of God to discover. Barrenness, like nothing else, reminded me how far I was from believing the truths about God that I proclaimed, how far I was from leaning against Him the way I wanted a baby to lean against me.

Yet He seemed to have ordained the emptiness every month's not-yet created in my understanding. He seemed to be in the hunger itself.

There has to be more here, I finally breathed, forehead to knees.

I barely know You, I whispered within, loosening my grip.

Bible-believing brothers and sisters stake their theological claims about healing all over the map, all over His Word. I've tried many of those theories on for size and am learning that the theologies that stand are those that are both rooted in His Word and not only said but worn. They foster new growth when everything you've preached is challenged underneath the skin of your life.

The question of pain, it's buried deep in my bones. It *is* my story, though I've barely traveled the circumference that others have, not even to the half. But God wants me to know the nearness of Him in response to the deepest questions of my story, the kind of nearness that, when realized, heals.

Many of us, with bodies broken, find comfort by accepting what we've loosely defined as God's sovereignty. After all, hope is awkward in a life of living by sight. It's messy. It's vulnerable.

At times it's easier to accept a diagnosis than to believe He can heal. To know Him as Healer requires me to be always asking. To know Him as Healer requires me to stay, longer than I'd like to, as one in need of healing.

For those of us wanting to escape the tension of hope, too often we cease to think of God's sovereignty as "He will decide" and instead come to think of it as "Here I am, forced into this position by a greater power."

My form of pain held a monthly reckoning with this question: What does God do when a body breaks? But God was healing me even while I waited on His healing.

When I asked, *How much of my broken body and broken life do I accept as lasting forever?* the God who is sovereign over my story whispered, *Be near to Me.* When I asked, *What if I pray, seek, and ask, and You don't heal me?* He answered with a dream for me that is far beyond what I'd whittled down for myself.

To know God as Healer is a relationship, not a moment. *Search Me out*, He says. *There is always more of Me to be found.*

I was awake while the rest of my household slept.

I stumbled out of bed and padded across the carpet into my own little sanctuary, the room off of our bedroom. I tucked my feet underneath me in my oversized chair, which was faded in spots from the sun, and pulled to my chin the winter blanket I wasn't ready to relinquish to spring.

I was raw and this was my safe place.

My awareness of my infertility was as variable as the rain. Some days it was a drizzle in the backdrop of my story, and other days it was a downpour altering my whole day.

This morning it was like that heavy rain. I'd gone to bed sad, and awakened while it was still dark, still sad. Years and hunger had allowed space for me to learn where to go when it rains like this.

The dialogue with God that started early in my married life out of necessity—I, without tools to face the gaps inside of me, standing before Him with all my uncertainty—continued and matured.

More recently, God had used Nate to give more shape to this conversation.

God was teaching me how a covenant relationship—

even one in which one or both parties are being pieced back together—can soothe decades of life's lacerations.

Over years of processing with Nate the hurt and pain of circumstances and people and the wounds we inflicted on one another, I'd developed a habit of conversation with him that went beyond simple requests and tasks. We learned to talk about hurts, not just react to them. What used to be minutes of catch-up chatting before bed grew to hours of diving into one another's worlds. We explored each other, with undiscovered frontiers still before us.

Nate had taught me how to sit on the Father's lap when pain left me desperate for an escape. I had practiced, with Nate, a way of talking with God that was both uncomfortable and exhilarating. I hadn't known God to engage in this way with the minutia of my life until I'd witnessed Nate's response to all that my pain was unearthing. As Nate had learned to respond carefully, softly, to the splinters in my heart and understanding (as he too practiced a new kind of love), I had begun to believe this might be a shadow of how God responds to my pain.

He'd told this mess of me that I am beautiful.

In this way, my walked-out experience with love began to match the God of Scripture I'd begun to adore.

Nate spoke of me as having a feminine softness long before I learned to express that quality. He'd grabbed another box of tissues and lived out patience while I learned to take emotional baby steps. "The Automaton," he used to call me early in our marriage. He had demonstrated pain as an opportunity.

God was overshadowing us.

So here I was, a decade later, wrapped up in my blanket, sinking deep into that sun-faded chair while the rest of the world slept, thinking of Nate still asleep in my bed, while being reminded that this sadness was serving a purpose. The chai might lift me for an hour, but God had a shift in mind for my heart.

I talked to my God like I talked to my husband.

I cried to Him, recounting events and asking His insight. I listened, quiet and expectant.

I curled up on His lap.

This was love. One long conversation, not interrupted by adversity but enhanced by it.

From this chair, communion was not only attractive; it was alluring. God leaned in to my broken body and called it beautiful.

Christmas Eve was days away. Our plan was to exchange gifts under low lights and in the Christmas tree's glow after the children were in bed. This tradition was my favorite. I treasured this night when Nate and I sat together under the mystery of the God-man and expressed our pale simile of His love.

It was a week before our second Christmas with Eden and Caleb when my monthly reminder of being a woman, a broken woman, was late. So I was a week "behind" with a budding promise of finally being the kind of "ahead" for which I'd longed for so many years. I started planning.

I would write a letter—Nate's love language—unveiling the secret I'd kept for a week on the same night that the secret Mary had kept hidden for nearly a year broke into the earth. It was hard to keep my mind from being consumed by these preparations.

The promise had finally come, I declared to my expectant spirit.

But Christmas Eve brought with it another message.

Hope deferred. Again.

I blushed at what no one but God had seen. I felt foolish. I had let myself go there again.

No letter for Nate. Now, only an explanation of why this once expectant day made me distant and pensive.

What was this all about?

Though my flesh might contrive that God was toying with me—a delay like this, resurrecting hope in an empty tomb—could there be yet more of Him to know?

I didn't know when I'd joined this group of women for a Bible study that my hot topic would be discussed. My posture changed when the instructor on the video began to talk about healing. We were only weeks into a yearlong study on Jesus in the Gospels, and the topic of healing was not one I expected on this particular day.

I slouched in my seat, alongside these unknowing women, and tried to hide my distress. How could I disguise what welled up within me whenever healing was brought up? The pain was too near to my very core.

I'd determined, early on, that the only people safe enough to advise me on healing were those, steeped in the Bible, who themselves knew daily what it is like to walk in a not-yet-healed body. This preemptive boundary was not healthy, or necessary, but I was wounded, and the wounded set up provisions for their comfort.

I quickly vetted this instructor to whom we all were tuning in, wondering if he'd had chronic pain or a child with a long-term illness or a disease that had crept into his family. Had he practiced his theology?

Later, I learned it didn't matter.

As he followed a tangent about Adam naming each of the animals — how he walked out a position of earthly authority while enjoying God's friendship — God imprinted something on my mind. A long awaited request — *God, make this information move my heart, not just open my mind* — received a response. I saw Adam in the flesh standing before a big God who was inviting his participation, and I related.

This wasn't just a nice story explaining how the earth first breathed and then others on it breathed too. Genesis provided a full-color account that filled one of the many holes in my understanding of God.

God shared His job.

He *partnered*.

"Out of the ground the LORD God formed every beast of the field and every bird of the air, and brought them to Adam to see what he would call them. And whatever Adam called each living creature, that was its name."

God spoke and it existed. Words and sentences formed continents and bodies of water and creatures. The great divides between heaven and earth and ocean and land were brought into being by a phrase on His lips. Not even one full page of words did it require for everything we know to be created.

Yet He gave Adam a role.

He waited on Adam to "see what he would call them."

Many times I'd read those words as if they were a historical account. One by one by one, those animals were given names. I pictured a roll call. *Bear, tiger, antelope, squirrel.*

But Adam was a boy-man, a son, created by God and walking in communion with the God who created Him. Instead of fielding orders and responding to commands, as I'd pictured him, Adam was invited into heavenly discourse.

His Father and Creator wielded words to make land and sea and sky. Bones snapped together and were clothed in flesh by just one phrase. Heaven had a voice.

God's words made life.

The man he formed with one sentence to bear His image and walk in perfect fear didn't just observe; he participated. Adam too had a voice. He painted color into the story—his colors, his choice. He did so with confidence, the kind of confidence that a son who knows he is loved, passionately, wears.

As this revelation moved from my mind to my heart, it touched the wound of years of speculating why my womb was hollow and how I was to respond to that hole. Before I could conceptualize this truth, my heart released a crying sigh. I began to weep. Right there in the Bible study, swallowing sobs. I saw another piece of faulty understanding of God fall away. (How many more could there be? Do I ever want this to end?)

I'd approached Him all these years on this one issue like the beggar I thought He'd made me to be, inconsequential and insignificant before Him. *Please God, please God.* I repeated words like rote religious petitions, stumbling over myself to get close to an answer, when the One giving the answer wasn't even in my picture. The One on the other end of my requests was behind guarded doors, doling out responses like Santa Claus. And I, apparently, had not been "nice." I prayed as one who believes she is cursed might pray.

"Overlooked" is how I had positioned myself before God, even long before my womb clamped shut. Overlooked is what made me pedal faster and harder in those years when I hoped my ministry might get His attention and, better,

His endorsement. Overlooked is what made me hide, lonely, under marriage's strain when my friends were in newly-wed bliss. After all, why should God notice someone who is cursed?

The habit of adoration, however, had introduced me to a new paradigm of inviting His words—true words, but new to me—to be written over these long-held false conceptions.

The newest frontier to be explored was my stance as I walked into the room of the God-man who had permitted my fertility's lengthy pause.

In that room I had seen myself as the beggar, unnoticed.

This one morning, however, as women who knew my name but not my story surrounded me, He revealed Himself as the One who gave authority to Adam, His created one, the son He loved not mildly but with passion.

My body heaved under the new picture of Him that He was imparting to me.

I didn't need to pound on the doors of heaven in the hope that some house steward might add my name to a list. I didn't need to recite my request over and over or hoist rocks over a high wall behind which a legion of servants might one day carry my petition to the King. Nor did I need to shrug at the lot I'd been cast, stretching wider Scripture's definition of sovereignty.

This request, around which my fingers had been clenched for years, was meant to be delivered palm to palm as I sat on His lap in confidence. I didn't need to whine or beg, as if I were a child used to hearing no. I needed to look up and say, "Father, would You grant my desire for a child to come from my womb?" My hands in His, together.

My figurative position of confidence before Him, as a daughter in whom He delighted, was one long exhalation of relief. I didn't earn this position; I *inherited* it, and that made my safety all the more secure, no matter His response. The ability He gave me to ask started, first, with Him.

From this angle, how could I not ask?

On that morning, I was Adam.

For Your Continued Pursuit

1 Samuel 16:7 | 2 Corinthians 12:8 – 9 | Proverbs 24:16 | John 15:11 – 13 | Romans 4:17 | Proverbs 18:21 | Genesis 2:19 | Acts 2:17 | Isaiah 51:3 | Matthew 8:16 – 17 | 2 Corinthians 1:3 | 1 Peter 1:3 | 2 Corinthians 4:16 – 18 | Matthew 7:7 – 8 | Psalm 34:18 | Psalm 71:5 | Proverbs 13:12 | Genesis 2:18 – 20 | Psalm 33:9 | 1 Peter 1:6 – 7 | Psalm 147:11 | Psalm 8:3 – 8

nine

LET US RUN TOGETHER

"He is not far from each one of us."

On the day we took Eden and Caleb back to visit their orphanage—a week after we'd wrapped them in jammies for the first time at the guesthouse—I saw a face I will never forget.

She was seven or eight—maybe a malnourished nine—and she held the babies with ease, as if they were her own children. She ushered us around the orphanage, a holding place for so many but a permanent home to her. This child was the welcoming committee for all the parents who came to adopt their babies from that place. Her smile was warm and inviting, but her eyes betrayed her. *Take me home*, they said.

It was clear she'd done this routine dozens of times, but familiarity didn't hide the longing underneath her role. She envied the babies she held, the ones to whose cribs were attached pictures of mommies and daddies in America, waiting to come get them. She wanted to crawl back into infant skin and be afforded their way out. She wasn't yet hopeless, but each time a family arrived for a child in diapers, she *yearned*. This baby's "homecoming" into their arms was a reminder to her of what she didn't have.

That girl came back with me, in my heart, from Ethiopia. Her face haunted my nights for months. *Who will teach her how to read a poem and show her how to paint a rainbow and tell her that He died for her?* I wondered.

"I know there is another for us," I told Nate after tucking Eden and Caleb in bed one night. We'd had no plans to adopt again, but I was hopeful that one of these forgotten ones, one of the many who lived orphanage life not as a transition but as a home, would find their way into our lives.

We had had Eden and Caleb home from Ethiopia for one year. They were three and a half and one and a half, respectively, when we got them, though their malnourished little frames and the language barrier made us feel as if we were raising two toddlers. The process to bring them home took years instead of the months we'd expected, but their transition into our family was relatively smooth. One year felt like four, and soon adopting again seemed more natural than it did challenging.

So we moved from conversation to filling out paperwork and writing a check. Nate and I both knew that the young caregiver we'd met in Ethiopia wouldn't be the child to come home with us—we weren't yet ready to adopt an older child—but it was her face that spurred us on. The one who longed. The one who was overlooked.

We decided on Uganda. Another African country seemed fitting, and we felt a nudge to pioneer a place that was relatively new to adoption. We acted like veterans as we prayed about this decision. Wasn't a year's experience with two little ones enough to call us knowledgeable? It wouldn't be long before we learned that experience doesn't translate into ease.

Our one nonnegotiable as we considered the age and gender of these next two children was that they both be younger than Eden. Though we hadn't leaned heavily on adoption literature as a guide, we'd heard enough negatives about trumping the birth order to decide this was not a move we wanted to make. Eden was clearly our oldest.

Wasn't she?

I sat before God just weeks after we'd signed the initial papers, asking for any bit of confirmation. Now that we were putting signatures behind the dream to adopt again, I was growing to realize the weight of what we'd just decided. One phrase came to me as I prayed: *It will be harder than your last adoption, but you will bring them home.* I didn't know what to make of this, so I logged it in my journal and knew that time would tell whether this was a nudge from Him.

Months passed like weeks and we received our first referral from our agency before we'd had time to begrudge the waiting process. We'd settled into a life of waiting to such a degree that when things moved quickly, we were surprised.

Her picture came into our inbox and we learned, then, that she was Eden's age. The first rule we'd erected was challenged, but when we tried her on in prayer, this one felt like she was ours. We rationalized: adopting a child the same age isn't quite as drastic as displacing Eden as the oldest.

We chose to name this little five-year-old Hope, and we waited on a referral for another, expecting it would come in the traditional way. During our wait, however, God surprised us again.

One Saturday morning, I received an email from someone who had read my blog. She told me of friends in Uganda who were nurses. Would we pray for them as God peppered their paths with the fatherless? Of course I said yes.

Nate and I prayed and immersed ourselves in the stories of

these two nurses and the children God had brought to their care. In one months' time, we learned of two children who lived at an orphanage just around the corner from them, needing a home.

Soon we learned, though, that those two little ones were points on our adoption map and not our destination. Their pictures had been plastered on our wall alongside the picture of Hope, who was also still waiting for us, but we would not meet them. Then one of the nurses said this: "But there's another."

A child, orphaned most of her life. But she wasn't the under-four boy we thought would be our next referral, or the toddler girl we pictured in our mix. We thought she might be seven, bordering eight, but couldn't be certain.

"It's too soon," Nate had said earlier when I proposed adjusting our age limitations. "We're still learning how to parent these two young ones. It's too early to introduce an older child."

I respected his reserve and deferred the image of that young Ethiopian girl for a later time and season. I knew she represented someone to me, but I trusted Nate's not-yet.

So when Nate stood in the kitchen just a few months later as we discussed this child of whom we'd just learned, the one who had shed diapers many years ago and likely had lost most of her baby teeth, I was not prepared for his response: "We have to go after her."

Something had shifted inside of him. He'd decided this child, this older child, would no longer be an orphan. She would be a Hagerty.

In just a few months' time, we'd moved from envisioning a family of children who were five and under to considering inviting a five-year-old and a seven- or eight-year-old into our fold, trumping the birth order twice over. Our family would grow up before it had even merged under our roof.

Months later, we sat over hotel food billed as "gourmet-local" and tried to pretend this anniversary weekend was lighter than it was. Having planned a few months in advance, we had no idea this forty-eight-hour stint away would be our weekend to settle on a decision that would impact the rest of our lives.

I scooted my food around my plate with my fork, shoulders slumped in fear.

"What are we doing?" I said. I really meant, "Who are we to do this?"

We were still considering the girl whose picture we'd received in our inbox, the same age as the girl we'd left behind at the orphanage in Ethiopia. Older. The kind many adoption experts say might take a decade or more to heal.

She felt safe as a hypothetical. Nate and I could still be like children, catching wind on the tire swing as we talked about lofty dreams and the days ahead when we'd leave our imprint on the world.

But when that hollow child had a name and a face and we had an opportunity, the world tilted for me. When Nate said, "We have to go after her," I froze.

I stood in a crazy nexus of desire and uncertainty. I wanted her. And my pulse quickened at the thought of seeing death and abandonment change to life and belonging in my home.

But she petrified me. She brought pain with her, unfamiliar pain, and wounds of the kind I'd not yet seen healed with my own eyes. A whole host of people whose stories of how life "went awry" after pursuing such a child echoed through my mind. All the statistics of older-child adoption I'd read ran like ticker tape in my thoughts. A new form of haunting.

Yet the husband who had once been not yet ready to pursue a child this broken was now saying yes.

What was holding me back? I had dressed for my funeral. My girlish dream, birthed years after my youth, to take her lanky arms and legs and wrap them up as infant in my fold now felt like a death sentence. Surely our lives would head downhill after taking on such a risk, I reasoned, fearing the worst, as was my tendency.

Our family at the time, freshly forged over only two years, felt rich. Eden and Caleb were a total delight, and the testimony we'd thought would take years to emerge was already a banner. We didn't know then that many of the wounds that had been inflicted before they could even talk wouldn't surface until years later. Parenting in this period of dormancy was by no means easy, but it was smooth. And we were crazy about them.

An older child threatened to disrupt the beauty that had finally settled over our broken years. I wanted to wrap my fingers around this new state and never let go.

As we discussed it over dinner and during walks and late-night ponderings, one thing became clear.

This wasn't about her. Nor was it about me or Nate or Eden or Caleb.

It was about Him.

Who was He—to me, to her, to our family?

Our conversation reminded me of the night I had awakened, alert, as if I'd never closed my eyes hours earlier. He was there, this firstborn child for whom we'd spent a decade praying.

Except I didn't see him; he was just a promise in a dream. For a few moments I got to live what I'd practiced in my mind through all these years of waiting.

But then a word, spoken over him, changed my hope of him in an instant. A "prophet" came and told me his life would be short lived. He would die of SIDS, this firstborn my womb longed to carry.

In the dream, I laughed, relieved. *Phew!* At least I knew in advance that this hope of my adult life, birthed, would crumble. I'd lived so many years fearing the worst that to have it be definitive — in my dream — brought relief to my sickened perspective.

In waking life, I knew the dream wasn't a foreshadowing, but something about it made me unable to shake it.

The memory of the dream surfaced again as Nate and I dissected my continued resistance to that seven-year-old girl in Uganda who still had life left in her eyes, though she had every reason to live out grief.

This time my confusion made me wonder whether the dream *was* a foreboding. *Is she the infant who died? Does God want to prepare me for the worst? What if we've gotten our hopes up, and her hopes up, only to have them vanish in the night? What if we've wrapped her in our story and it isn't her story to live? What if we've made a mistake?*

David had a son once. He too heard from a "prophet": "the child who is born to you shall surely die."

Did he laugh like me in that dream? Did his lungs inhale the air of relief? Was he grateful that he was made ready for the worst?

No. He pleaded and he fasted. He fought.

He didn't wrap the blanket of circumstances around

himself, even those circumstances he deserved. Instead, he beseeched God.

Though the child died, David was still the one whom the all-knowing God had called "a man after my own heart."

I'd grown comfortable bracing myself for the worst. It felt safe this way. Though some layers of this negativity had been shed over the years, it still had a hold on my soul.

It's true that God had begun to hem Job's message into me: "the Lord gives and the Lord takes away." I said those words out loud. I wrote them. I whispered them to myself as finances and friendships and dreams fell on the chopping block in our lives. But still it felt easier to gird up under the taking away. Just in case.

And so she had to be fought for, not just for her but for me. Once again a point of decision had more to do with my perspective on God's goodness than anything else.

Could I move forward with hope, not tentatively but boldly, joyfully?

Hunger had carved a space for me not just to commune with Him but also to clasp hands and run with Him.

Lily would be my escort.

For Your Continued Pursuit

James 1:27 | 2 Samuel 12:1–20 | 1 Samuel 13:14 | Acts 13:22 | Job 1:21 | Lamentations 3:24–26 *ten*

HOLD ALL OF ME

"For we were saved in this hope."

And so we told her—through papers and phone calls and emails, as if we could will her to know our love across so many messengers and miles—that we were coming. We would bring her home along with her new sister, Hope. Having made our decision, we settled into the process.

Then Nate came home from a morning prayer meeting and said, "I think we need to go to Uganda—now."

My heart slumped. It was as if I'd lost nine years' worth of marital work in nine seconds. Back again to newlywed, when I was nearly heart-dead from placing the same boundaries of control on Nate that I'd placed on myself.

"Now?" I said. Although my four-page trip-prep checklist was nearly complete, we still had no sign of a court date, and the Ugandan courts closed in about three weeks for a long summer recess. If we went now, we chanced staying months in-country and taking on all of the emotional and financial expenditures of raising a family of four (make that six) in temporary living quarters.

I grilled him.

Why now? Where did this thought come from? Was this direction from God or just a boyish craving for adventure?

The truth is nothing about adoption is safe. We sign papers

---

ten

HOLD ALL OF ME

"For we were saved in this hope."

And so we told her—through papers and phone calls and emails, as if we could will her to know our love across so many messengers and miles—that we were coming. We would bring her home along with her new sister, Hope. Having made our decision, we settled into the process.

Then Nate came home from a morning prayer meeting and said, "I think we need to go to Uganda—now."

My heart slumped. It was as if I'd lost nine years' worth of marital work in nine seconds. Back again to newlywed, when I was nearly heart-dead from placing the same boundaries of control on Nate that I'd placed on myself.

"Now?" I said. Although my four-page trip-prep checklist was nearly complete, we still had no sign of a court date, and the Ugandan courts closed in about three weeks for a long summer recess. If we went now, we chanced staying months in-country and taking on all of the emotional and financial expenditures of raising a family of four (make that six) in temporary living quarters.

I grilled him.

Why now? Where did this thought come from? Was this direction from God or just a boyish craving for adventure?

The truth is nothing about adoption is safe. We sign papers

125

and write checks and make timelines as if any part of this process is secure, and then we're shocked when the battle waged in the heavens over these children's lives encompasses the natural.

The fields of the fatherless are war stained.

I forgot about that when Nate suggested doing the unconventional. *He's crazy*, I thought.

So we got down on our faces. I, asking for confirmation. Nate, balancing the certainty of what he thought we were to do and his wife's hesitations.

Once again, God gave me opportunities to advance. To see the strength in this man I was given in the same way He sees the beauty in this weakhearted woman who was Nate's bride. Because really, every issue in my marriage can find its source in a rift between Nate or me and our heavenly Father.

Six days and ten bags later, we left. Our lawyer said, "Don't come." Our agency said, "Don't go." Both were certain that we faced three or more months in-country, because there was "no way" we'd get into court before the summer recess. But my insecure heart chose to follow the lead of the man He had given me. I'm pretty sure I had missed many opportunities to practice trust, but something inside of me said, *It's not too late*.

"Jesus told me they were coming," she said to the woman who confirmed the news a day later. She knew before she was told that her day had come. Her family had arrived.

We watched on the steps of our guest home for the gates to open to the car delivering her. It was the day after we'd arrived in Africa. Kampala's sky had set too early for my liking, but God knew this holy moment needed a curtain of privacy. My family waited in the dark for this baby to crown, and I sensed the aroma of God filling the birthing room.

The car came to a halt just long enough for us to hear her squeal from inside: "Daddy!"

Lily launched out of the car, and in seconds (after joyful acknowledgment of her new siblings) she found herself no longer fatherless and in the arms of her earthly daddy. Such a picture to me, that lanky seven-year-old with her legs wrapped around his waist and her arms clasped behind his neck as if to say, *Hold my story, Daddy. Hold all of me.*

Even in that moment, the release of the months of waiting to brush my fingers along Lily's skin brought with it the weight of reality.

I was being entrusted with a life, broken, in the midst of my own healing.

I wasn't ready.

I wasn't ready to cup my hands around a face malnourished from touch and be her emotional IV drip. *Babies raising babies* is what I felt then and in the days that followed.

Lily's adoption was a glorious mix of human desires and God's strong hand to raise them up. I too was growing to be a confident child, eyes wild and cheeks flushed by the delight of my Father, sitting on His lap and asking big things of Him.

Even with all the waiting and changing behind me, I was just beginning my pursuit of this beautiful girl, just beginning my pursuit of all His new frontiers.

And Hope? When we chose her name, we had a two-dimensional version of her in our inbox, accompanied by four sentences. I sat on the bed, computer in front of me and heart racing, ready to absorb everything about this child, who might just be *our* child.

Three of the four sentences spoke of what she *didn't* have, not who she was: she was clear of HIV, fatherless, and without a real home. Even her picture was indistinct; she still wore the uniform of the orphanage where she lived.

Buried in those words was the only information we had on her personality: "She is a very active girl."

And so like every parent, we chose a name knowing only a gender and that this child could kick.

"Hope," we decided, as we drove across the Kansas plains with the Rockies at our backs on a family vacation, just days after seeing her picture on our screen. The barrenness that winter had left behind seemed an appropriate backdrop to this name, one that was more about us than it was about her, at least at the time.

This was our year to hope, to walk away all filled up with what His Word tells us doesn't disappoint. We were choosing His storyline over our circumstances, having had a small taste that circumstances look a whole lot different when He overshadows.

Her name was an extension of us, of His work in us. We didn't yet know that this semicasual pick was perfect, both for who she was and what she would become. Her name would be our signpost.

Five months later, I saw Hope for the first time. It was the day after Lily barreled out of the car and into Nate's arms. We pulled up to Hope's orphanage and were swarmed by those who'd shared bedrooms and lunches and playtimes with her. They knew more of her than her picture and those four sentences.

She fumbled nervously over the doll we brought her, shyly relieved to look at something, anything, other than us. I kissed her cracked and soiled skin as if it were baby soft. Most five-year-olds aren't pushed into becoming a daughter to strangers in one day. We cloaked any awkwardness we may have felt with overstated warmth, seeking to ease her nerves. But hope had already been doing its work.

She led us around the orphanage proudly, anxious to show us her bed. I wondered how long she'd spent smoothing out the creases of the covers, knowing we were coming. While she boasted in her native tongue about the care she'd taken with her bedspread, my eyes fixed on the only sprig of light in that drab room. Amid grays and blues and browns, hers was the one bedspread in the room that had color. It was also the only one that had words: "Hope It's Happy," it read.

We hadn't told her yet of her new name, but she'd been sleeping under it for months. He was speaking over her even then.

Hope had done what it always does: it preceded us.

The days that followed revealed this child to be a bit more than just "very active." Nerves from a life lived long on the streets kept her from slowing down.

"Catch me, Daddy!" she cried across the field in heavily accented English, as she darted out of sight when Nate said, "Come here." Love in any form made her run. She proudly wore the label "mischievous" that one caregiver had given her.

When Nate held her tight and whispered other words—"I love you. You are my daughter"—Hope's formerly fatherless self vomited on his chest. Her body and soul weren't ready to handle another's arms. In the face of the love, unbroken, that we continued to pour out alongside her misbehavior, she crumbled.

But God gives life to the dead. He calls things that are not, as though they are.

Weeks later, in a casual conversation while still in Uganda, we learned that Hope didn't have a surname when she entered the orphanage. Before she knew of us—and before they knew of us—they had assigned her the Luganda name *Suubi*.

It means "hope."

The Lord had been rewriting her story even before we arrived in it.

Now He was asking us to participate, because the Word dwells among us and takes on flesh. We would wear hope in Him, for her, just as she wore her name. We would behold Him as the one who *enjoys* when we hope, who positions us, daily, to live in hope.

We also learned when our Hope was born. It was the same month God had once promised me a child, the same month Eden was born: September 2005.

We'd been in Uganda two days, Lily and Hope were in our arms, and we were off to the paperwork races. We knew our early arrival meant forfeiting the traditional adoption in-country experience. The work that normally would be done before we came, arriving in time to enjoy a casual, cultural experience while adjusting to our children, was work we'd now do ourselves.

Long days and into the nights, we found ourselves traveling the rock-ridden roads of Uganda chasing paper. Our kids, old and new, made beds at our feet and drooled over themselves in sleep, folded up in all sorts of angles in the car that held this craziness.

We were all tired.

This certainly wasn't how I'd envisioned our first days as a family of six.

Africa witnessed some of my weakest moments. I stretched to believe in bureaucratic and logistical miracles on little sleep, with obstacles confronting us every day. Long hours in the soft prayer room off my bedroom, my feet slippered and a cup of tea in my hand, would have made it a lot easier to pray clearly into what felt like chaos.

My flesh was taut around my circumstances, but my heart was being given opportunity to grow.

On one particular day, we had decided to file our case with the court system in one of our children's villages. We were tight for time. Courts closed in two days for the remainder of the summer season. To get a court date assigned within this two-day window was unheard of. To not get a court date assigned within this two-day window meant a few months longer—at least—in Uganda.

We left the capital city of Kampala an hour later than we expected. This was early, for Africa time. We had a multiple-hour drive in front of us, and though the road was paved, our bodies rocked and bumped as if we were on a rickety old roller coaster. My hair stuck to the back of my neck, and I sweated in my court clothes. We chattered away as if this were any old day, but I knew that the hourglass was almost empty on the Ugandan business day, our last day to make our miracle request that our case be heard in court the next day.

Those days in Uganda, I lived out of my heart, not my head, purely as survival. If I'd had any time to analyze the events unfolding and our prayers for the impossible, I would have quickly rationalized myself out of hope. But the gift of

God was that very weakness, my flesh stretched thin to the tearing point. Sleep deprivation and flash-pot circumstances, ever changing, didn't afford me much time for reason.

Our driver knew our hurry and had, himself, become invested in an outcome. But thirty minutes outside of the village, he swerved to the side of the road and launched out of the car. He scratched his head and was joined by our lawyer, who was also wearing court clothes in preparation for making his absurd request seem normal in court.

Flat tire.

Roadside assistance service doesn't exactly exist in the bush.

I looked at my watch and absorbed what this flat tire meant. Not only would missing this chance at a court date mean spending the summer trying to forge a family in a guest home, but every month longer meant a deeper slide into the perplexing abyss of international adoption. Adoptive parents pray their children home because they know that any day the doors on the adoption policies of their children's countries could shut.

We stood staring at our predicament.

Schoolchildren passed us, chanting in a foreign tongue, uniforms stained and eyes revealing a life lived long in their short years. Gray-haired men pumped the pedals of bicycles carrying women sitting sidesaddle. People on motorcycles— *boda bodas*, they're called here—streaked past without giving us a second look.

I dialed the number of the one friend we knew in Uganda. I couldn't get the words off my tongue before I heard, "Wait, is that you?" She wasn't asking if that was my voice; she was asking if that was my *car*, in front of her, on the road.

The bus carrying her and another family headed to this

same remote village pulled up behind us, as if we were suburban neighbors just passing by.

This happenstance didn't register as rare until I climbed onto their bus with one child on my hip and another child's hand wrapped in mine. (This was the bus they "weren't sure why" they felt they needed to rent that morning, and the only vehicle that could have carried all of us.) I hadn't even had time to shed tears over our delay before God had provided a response.

We held hands with these people and poured out gratitude to the God who had become our backup plan before we'd even mustered breath to ask. We were still letting the miracle sink in as the bus pulled into the courthouse parking lot before the sun set on that day.

So often, I envision warring alongside God hand in hand, mutual contributors to a great work of glory.

But Uganda left me without abilities. I stumbled and tripped and floundered my way into every African miracle—and there were many.

It wasn't my effort and His. It was His effort and my weak yes.

It was partnership, done His way.

I couldn't boast of how I'd earned this series of miracles or won His favor by my fervor. He saw all my foibles. Morning, noon, and night knew my repentance. There was no hiding my weakness when the power was out again, when we had standing water in the bathroom, when my food swarmed with ants and my children were desperate for the sleep and routine that our unforgiving schedules did not allow.

Every time we faced a setback, His response astounded us.

I had a side of God to witness anew in Africa.

The One who fights for me.

The One who covenants with me and wraps the strength of Himself like a seal around that covenant.

The One who simply asks for my yes.

And so I too was being pursued.

God would use adoption to Father me.

During our first adoptions, of Eden and Caleb, I'd nearly collapsed under every delay. Angry and frustrated, cursing the enemy-thwarter and driving harder at each roadblock, I couldn't find relief. *They were made to be in my home!* was the line that overtook any deeper work God was doing in me. I pushed. I pressed. All toward the goal of bringing them home. That *was* the goal, wasn't it? That was the singular storyline? Rescue. Redemption. Restoration. All for the child.

With our adoptions of Lily and Hope, their deep wounds alone were what threatened to lure me into their storyline. But this wasn't just about God healing *them*. I would be a recipient of His work as well. The pain and hurdles of my most stunning quest—adoption—were also parts of my heart knowing hunger. If hunger won out, I just might receive new perspective. I just might grow.

I assumed, again, that growth would come through disappointment, not fulfillment. When we made plans to leave for Uganda on a week's notice, I had to face the likelihood that a hasty departure could mean forfeiting the first family beach trip since my dad had died. I couldn't even talk about this possibility without tears. This was my dad's legacy trip. Though he wouldn't be there to participate, the tradition was golden to me.

We left, and I prayed the impossible to the God who, I

sensed, kept saying, *Ask of Me what you want*. This phrase fell counter to how I'd figured God to be in the past. It pushed me, again, to consider how I'd envisioned myself as His daughter. Not just in my infertility but also in how I approached this adoption and all of its uncertainties, God was stretching me to approach Him as a daughter whose desires matter to Him.

Resting in the back of my mind was a dream my Lily had shared with her foster mom, months earlier. She dreamed that she was on the beach with her mommy and daddy.

"But then I woke up," she said. She found herself still underneath Ugandan bedcovers.

When her foster mom shared this with me over email while we waited to come get the girls, I wondered, *Is He whispering an early promise of something that seems impossible to her—and to me?*

Dry, dusty Africa was quickly becoming the land of miracles for me. I'd never seen so many "impossibles" come together. God's fight for our little girls was remarkable.

We had packed for the potential of staying six months or more, but less than six weeks into our trip, we received a positive ruling from the judge for both Lily's and Hope's cases.

Weeks after arriving in-country, we found ourselves at the embassy collecting our final paperwork with the chance of making the one flight out in early August that had seats for all of us. We would either catch that flight or one nearly three weeks later—after my dad's legacy trip.

Two days before our scheduled departure, we went, weak kneed, to the embassy, praying that the girls' visas would be ready in time. Not one of our necessary adoption steps had fallen into place as planned. We had no logical explanation for how we'd even gotten this far. God was our story—the whole story, the only story.

As I cracked open the door to the waiting room with hardback chairs and a British news station playing only sound and no picture from the television, I walked with a new kind of confidence. A Spirit-led confidence I'd found on those barren African roads.

Five days into our trip, I had known I wouldn't come home the same. Five weeks in, approaching a new office with the same impossible story, I wore an expression that bubbles up from a new understanding.

It had always been safer to expect that God allows suffering in the interest of refinement. While I still believe this is a significant aspect of His nature, Uganda had given me the chance to discover new frontiers of His generosity. For He also allows joy.

Yes, the odds were against an August return. But the odds were no longer what gave my heart stability.

Endurance was producing character. Character was becoming hope.

I walked into the embassy, expectant.

As we waited, Nate, who finds a friend in any stranger, struck up a conversation with a British gentleman and his American wife, who were also waiting for an appointment.

When it was our turn, we discovered that the medical reports for Lily and Hope, necessary for our visas, had never arrived. The chances of our making the August flight were now very slim.

I felt tears flooding my eyes.

A day earlier, we'd moved our flights from on-hold to in-hand (spending our last funds in the process). "In faith," we'd said, knowing that the Father determines the outcome.

Standing in the embassy, I asked Him, *Which way do I pray?*

Do I lean in, still expectant, or do I accept this and praise You in the delay?

After our appointment, Nate commiserated with the strangers-turned-friends. The wife quietly jotted Lily's and Hope's names on a piece of paper. This I didn't notice. A friend who was with us noted it later as we retold the story.

While Nate was waiting to pay the cashier for services not yet rendered, he casually asked his new friend what exactly he did for the nonprofit organization he'd described. The man stumbled over his words to admit what he had concealed minutes earlier.

"Actually, well ... I'm the Head of Mission for the medical facility where your children's reports seem to have been lost. I plan to make a phone call when I leave here," he said.

Before close of business that very day, this man found the reports that a contract employee had misplaced. The next morning, they were couriered to the embassy so that our visas could be processed.

The following break of dawn, we were at the airport, visas in hand.

We lugged ten bags up the stairs of the airport entrance. Each one was a reminder: from each season emerges a new side of God. This was our time to know Him as the One who fights for us, the One who fights with us.

A week later, my little girl smelled saltwater for the first time.

She found herself at the beach, just as in her dream. Her daddy taught her how to ride the waves just as mine had taught me. I swallowed hard as I watched small pieces of her receive the breath of life under her own father's instruction.

I saw the powerful work of His hand, and His delight in hearing His children laugh.

For Your Continued Pursuit

Ephesians 5:25 | Psalm 89:13 | Romans 5:5 | Romans 4:17 | John 1:14 | Romans 8:24–25 | Romans 15:13 | Matthew 19:26 | 2 Corinthians 12:9–12 | Genesis 18:14 | Deuteronomy 1:30 | Genesis 17:7 | Romans 10:9 | Romans 8:15 | Galatians 4:6 | Matthew 7:7 | Matthew 21:22 | Romans 5:3–5

eleven

NEW NAMES

"Can these bones live?"

When we first pursued this second set of adoptions, I'd nearly forgotten my vision of a girl crawling to me across the bed. It wasn't long after we were home and medical tests confirmed Lily's age that I realized Lily was that toddler. She would have been one, just as I pictured her, at the time I saw her in my mind's eye.

God gave me a window into the years I didn't see, for just a moment. He seared my imagination with His, for me.

As we settled into our full house, my life's question was not just for my story anymore. Our second adoptions had brought a child approaching a decade of pain without a mommy and a daddy. In her hunger, in her barrenness, in her waiting for healing, was He good to *Lily?*

Months before, I had received a portentous text message from a friend. We were a season away from leaving for Uganda to get Lily and Hope. We hadn't even seen Lily's picture yet or imagined who she might be.

I was climbing into bed, eyelids heavy. The adoption process we'd begun meant lots of late-night email correspondence and prayers in the wee hours of the morning. Like a woman whose body is preparing to introduce the world to her child,

EVERY BITTER THING IS SWEET

and her child to the world, I was attuned to any of the "baby's" movements.

The text woke me up.

My friend in Virginia had sent verses, with little explanation. They were impressed on her for us. For now. For this child, or these children, who would soon be ours.

It was a passage from Ezekiel 37 that I'd read many times, but never in this light. God gave Ezekiel a vision of a valley of dry bones and told him to speak life to them. This man of dust became man of God as he spoke what was not into being. The bones came together and gained flesh. They breathed, they received God's Spirit, and they became warriors.

These words about Israel were also for me.

God said to Ezekiel, said to Israel, and whispered to me through my friend that night:

> They indeed say, "Our bones are dry, our hope is lost, and we ourselves are cut off!" Therefore prophesy and say to them, "Thus says the Lord GOD: 'Behold, O My people, I will open your graves and cause you to come up from your graves.'"
>
> —Ezekiel 37:11–12

Those bones were my children. Arid, barren, disconnected from their source, hopeless, but offered flesh by one word from a weak person representing a strong God.

I was called to be that weak one. Not only to believe but to speak His promises, despite what my eyes and my mind might tell me.

Weeks later, we learned of Lily. Months later, I held her for the first time.

She revealed herself, early on, as that dessicated valley of bones.

Her heart was waiting to be breathed upon. Emotional muscles present from birth, but without shape, had atrophied. Years spent existing, but not really living, had wearied her on the inside. And all of this bolstered my greatest fears.

Can He heal even her? Is she forever damaged?

Will these dry bones breathe?

She was starved, not even knowing she was hungry.

A week after Lily first came through those guesthouse gates, we took her back to visit the orphanage where she'd lived for years. We wanted her to have a sense of closure. We wanted to see where she had grown to be who she was so far.

I held her tight the whole way there, not knowing what a seven-year-old's response might be to revisiting the life she once wore. I wanted her body to retain the marks of a mother's arms as she reentered, for a few moments, the fields of the fatherless.

When we arrived at her orphanage, what seemed like one hundred children swarmed our *boda bodas*. She had been one of them, just days before, but she looked confused as she scanned the curious faces.

Soon, though, she found her friend, Stella, one of only two friends I'd heard her mention by name. I wondered, *Is it typical for an orphan not to have many friends, or is this her survival mechanism to see people as indistinct, to not attach?* She and Stella ran off together like carefree schoolgirls, which gave me time to take in the surroundings.

The children in the dirt yard played chase not much

differently than those here stateside tramping around our Western outdoor candy lands. Their eyes danced and their mouths squealed. *What is keeping them from paralyzing grief over their destitution?* I could barely face it. But these little ones had no option to look away. They were living it.

The pain stung even more at the thought of Lily's years lived so hungry while her mommy and daddy had abundance. Love ran free from the staff to the children, but those children's bellies were empty.

One small child, with flies swarming around his face, approached us with a concoction he'd made in the lid of a plastic bottle. My friend who was with me, who knew the child well from her months in-country, took a whiff and said, "No more, not good to eat."

What makes something good or bad to eat when you have no food?

I found Lily again—she'd seemed to recover a bit of herself—and asked her to show me her room. She'd forgotten where it was, though she had spent years in that bed. So Stella led us to the long, narrow dormer.

The dank space housed a corridor of beds, the path between the beds and the wall only wide enough for one person to pass. The cement walls were stained reddish brown with African soil, and the mattresses, some without sheets, sagged below wooden bunk frames. The thick smell of soiled beds and dirty clothes hung in the air. Only the door carved into a wall of cement afforded any light.

These living quarters were the intersection of childlike wonder and cold, hard loss. To Lily, this was now her past. To Stella, it was still her life.

I forced myself to look, to grasp at Lily's history. *Will*

her heart one day feel sick, as mine does now, over the gaps in her childhood?

Back home, I paged through Lily's prayer journal and found a spring amid what appeared to be a mostly arid existence. Lily didn't yet know who she was, but she seemed to know who did. She conversed with God in ways she couldn't converse with me.

I cried when I found her request that we come before the courts closed, to wait with her while the judge said yes.

"Answer my prayers, oh God," she wrote.

He did.

Now, with us, vacancy crept in behind her eyes during the moments when her sisters' giggles or Caleb's hugs didn't distract her. She stood shocked by every experience we introduced. Riding our bikes to get ice cream, building sandcastles, and cuddling at bedtime all elicited the same stunned response. It was clear she couldn't quite figure out how to fit her story into this new reality.

We took walks and read stories at night, and I held all of her tall, slender frame like she was a baby, praying for the right time to ask questions of her heart.

"It was good!" she said, many times, of her life before us. "Good" seemed to be the trap door between her head and her heart that had never been opened. There was little hint of her pain over her lost years.

"She's delightful," people told us again and again. And she was. She said and did all the right things.

But my mama's eyes saw empty, saw hunger. Saw bones in need of flesh.

⚭

Lily and her friend, Stella — once bunkmates and classmates — became pen pals. Stella had shared most of Lily's story with her. Together they knew a secret sisterhood of hollow years that few would ever understand.

Stella's future held less promise than that of almost all the other children in the orphanage. She was close to aging out. What happens to the fatherless when society wants to make them young fathers and mothers?

Her letters to Lily months after the girls said goodbye revealed her world, her very small world. "The orphanage received new mattresses!" she bubbled. She wrote of educational advancement within the orphanage and school testing and food.

Then in one letter came a cryptic postscript. "P.S. God gave me the new name Sarah." One small line, an afterthought.

I pondered this for months. Stella had innocently, almost matter-of-factly, accepted a name change from God. How did His words come to her — in prayer, in dreams, in play?

The orphan story is the extreme version of my pain — of our pain. Abandonment. Rejection. Loss. For some, a lifetime of loss. It is pain without an obvious answer, without an obvious explanation.

Children who live immersed in this pain grow numb to it. The flat expressions of many orphans is a reflection of being numb to hope as well. They know perhaps more than any of us that hope can be dangerous.

What does God say about that aging pain?

He says what He said to Stella.

He says, "Sarah."

Not *Sarai*, her old name, but *Sarah*, a new name to signify the covenant, the promise that He held for her. She was now bound. To Him. Everyone who spoke her new name made homage to hope. His destiny became her destiny. Her barrenness was buried in His promise.

My thoughts about her—Abraham's Sarah, or Lily's pen pal across the ocean, or my former orphan down the hall—reveal my thoughts about Him. If He is healer to me, restorer of all that is broken, I will see her not by her present loss, her forever fragmentation, but as Sarah. As one promised. As one chosen to carry His seal.

The brokenness at my dinner table and the even starker darkness across the ocean invites a God who gives new names.

This is the God I want to know. The One who named her Sarah.

On our beach trip soon after we returned home, we were swimming in the ocean when a quick head count at the shore revealed that Lily was missing.

I scanned the beach, feeling panic rise in the back of my throat. Back and forth, my eyes darted from the houses, the dunes, the ocean at our feet. I finally spotted her a few hundred yards down the beach, walking away from us. I ran to catch up with her, no idea where she was going.

When I reached her with my arms (because even calling her name didn't get a response), I saw that she was clutching her shoulder, stumbling over depressions in the sand. She didn't want to tell me what hurt, but she couldn't hide it. I finally pulled it out of her: she'd been stung by a jellyfish.

At first, I wasn't sure how to respond. What child runs

away from—not to—her mama when life hurts? Unlike my other children, she didn't clasp hands around my neck and cry into my chest with the expectation that Mommy or Daddy always finds a way to fix everything. She went cold. Distant. Minutes before, she'd been splashing saltwater all over her siblings. In pain, she became a stranger.

Mommy wasn't a healer in her story; Mommy was absent.

I saw myself in her. Even with these four beautiful ones in my home, I still waited for healing. I still longed. I still guarded myself, at times, against God's no.

I know, child, I wanted to say. *To ask for healing, for comfort, is dangerous. It's vulnerable. It feels easier right now to be alone. But I want you to look into my eyes and learn who I am, when you are hurt, so that you can come to me first.*

The lingering gaps in my life kept me close to God, as He wanted. As I wanted the chasms in Lily to keep her close to me. God never intends for us to ask, *Who are You in this pain?* only once. He wants us to make a habit out of coming near. Because His response to our pain will be safe.

Later I thought about my ache to hold Lily that day. I realized that if, at eighty, my body hasn't known the healing of the Sarah who went before me those thousands of years ago, I will know that I pleased Him with a hope that kept me raw and vulnerable to His touch.

The barrenness I shared with my children would serve a purpose, a holy purpose. He wants us to run toward Him, in expectation, when we are stung.

"You're a bad, bad mommy," she said with her words, after hours of saying it with her scowls and her shoulder shrugs. Last night's mommy-daughter time escaped her. Today's cuddles and words of encouragement, forgotten.

It hadn't taken long for this daughter to find enough comfort in our home to let what simmered, beneath, come up and out. Her pain was aimed at me: "I want to be in charge of myself!" Every word spoke two desires: *Go away, abandon me like I deserve!* and *Please don't leave me, Mommy.*

I reached out for her chin, searched behind those eyes, dark with years of secrets, and said His tender words, imparted, "Your sin isn't strong enough to push me away. Here is where my love for you grows. I will never stop loving you."

Later, Nate whispered to me behind closed doors, "She's no different than you once were, not too long ago."

Then I saw: there is a beauty in getting to live your story twice.

Those years of hunger, perplexity, and pain could now be found in these four little former orphans under my roof. Could I reach down into their pain to call forth the kind of hunger God had given me? Could we be the ones to teach them that He fills our barrenness?

Adoption invited a partnership with God in which we could express the new dimensions of Him that He had been revealing to us. The Father redeemed our story with the breath of His Word and then allowed us to walk it out again, with them.

I wondered if Adam thought about this during those simple days of beauty in the garden. He had received the Father's special benediction over his life ("it is *very* good"), and then he was invited to offer his own voice of blessing. He was even granted the privilege of naming his wife (Genesis 2:23).

As I began to see the shadows of my story in the hearts of

EVERY BITTER THING IS SWEET

my children, I lived my Father's kindness to me once more. I received His Word, even as I offered my own voice to bring forth life.

For Your Continued Pursuit

Ezekiel 37:11–12 | Genesis 17:15 | Song of Solomon 8:6 | 2 Corinthians 1:21–22 | Isaiah 42:3 | Hebrews 11:6 | Isaiah 54:1–8 *twelve*

THE GLORIOUS MUNDANE

"Your Father who sees in secret."

We were already twenty minutes behind schedule when the third issue surfaced in the third child. The prayer and writing room off of my bedroom had become a center for counseling that morning. Each time I walked out of my bedroom, I found another heart gone awry. Big tears on little faces, each child acting unraveled as if forever.

I was still unshowered, of course.

I didn't have long enough to feel exasperated before I heard, "Mommy?!"

A confused call from downstairs that got progressively louder as Lily reached the spot where I held her sister's newly confessed angst.

"The water isn't coming out of the faucet. Again."

I knew what had happened. Now being twenty minutes late and unshowered felt small. I let go of the latest hand I'd been holding and hurtled down two flights of stairs to find what I'd suspected, only worse. The water filter tank, suspended below the sink and over our keepsakes in the basement storage room, had fallen from its holding place in the rafters.

I'd thought we'd secured it.

Water dripped onto a collection of precious items, all organized on a table and ready to be inserted into what passed for the "baby books" of these ones we never saw as babies. The unkempt table had already been a reminder that I was behind my schedule for getting organized, even before the water filter fell on it.

The hearts that had lined up for mending an hour previously were now no longer urgent—to me—as I gathered towels to mend this spill that was seeping into some of the only pieces of their history we had.

All this before 9:00 a.m.

These bursts of chaos, amid cycle after cycle of laundry and dishes cleaned only to be made dirty again, make life for an ordered person feel constantly unsettled.

I'd known the pain of loss, the pain of not-yet, but I hadn't predicted the pain of motherhood's mundane demands.

I felt as if I couldn't possibly find peace, here, stuck between the numbing repetition of caregiving and the pandemonium of growing life, but could these moments, too, be purposed for great glory?

Even in the joy of our new family, the daily reality of living as a mama to four weighed heaily on me. We were stretching our family's new flesh across a midriff that felt tight. I talked to friends and debriefed with Nate through this lens: *It's just sinking in how hard it is to have four former orphans to raise. Four kids to raise, period, is a lot. I'm just overwhelmed by life.*

I nursed these thoughts and blamed my daily anxiety on the new clamor of my days. I found myself rushing through each day to get to my pockets of time away. I counted down from Friday until the next Thursday, as if awaiting a promised package on my doorstep: *Four afternoon hours to myself while Nate mans the fort.*

I made lists and cleaned corners, seeking to restore even just a remnant of my formerly ordered life. I put the children to bed early in the hope of getting more hours of "me time" back. I daydreamed about the magical "six months from now" when we would (I was sure) achieve a new normal as a family. I was scratching my skin raw, thinking that this new layer of fuller mommyhood was my true struggle.

Until I had a more accurate look.

My motherhood wasn't the source of my discomfort, and my children weren't its cause. My heart was detached. This was not a new truth, just a new setting in which it was revealed.

I was detached from Him, here.

I was believing the great lie of motherhood (which is likely the great lie of any busy life): *I'll find Him when life slows down or this burden lifts or my present struggle no longer nips at my heels.* Even if I didn't express those words, my actions and thoughts showed that I thought they were true.

Pain takes all sorts of shapes.

But all of these colliding circumstances—the children, the timing, the calling, the feelings that surfaced within me— were aligned for a purpose. To wait to seek Him when my load lifted—when these children weren't so needy, when I finally got on top of the laundry or was able to get a meal out on time—meant that I would miss the precise moment He'd ordained for me to find Him. Now.

The truth is that the battle in my life as a mother has rarely, if ever, been to find time for a twenty- or sixty-minute stint with my Bible cracked open and pen in hand. Instead, the fight is to find Him when the dishwasher breaks and a friend just doesn't understand me and my daughters' wounds surface again.

I can show up, morning after morning, for a designated "quiet time" with the Lord, without fail, but when my feet hit the stairs for the breakfast roundup, the barriers between me and the God-man appear.

Hiding beneath the disruptions is a battle keeping me from the minute-by-minute communion that makes me alive. My heart pushes back against the potential spiritual adventures of these moments.

I am hungry, again. I need Him, here, in this gap. I need to remember that God's answer is not to lift me out of "the crisis of the moment" but to speak His Word into it, and over it. I was made to find joy in relating to Him across the whole span of my day. That joy begins in knowing who He is.

Once again, adoration acquaints me with Him. The same habit of looking up that drew me to God in our prechildren days—when finances and marital pain were causing both the chaos and my distant stance toward God—causes me to adore that same God again. But I am a different worshiper, in a different season, wanting to understand once more why adoring Him is fuel for my life.

So after stumbling hundreds of times, I am learning the art of getting back up. For me that means showing up. It means choosing each day that I will adore Him in any pocket of time I can find. If (and when) I fail, I press delete and declare that moment a new day.

I will adore.

The psalmist says, "And I will look up," and I say yes to this with my minutes. When, even just for a moment, I take my eyes off of me and let them gaze deeply into God's eyes, life looks different. I can approach a plate of spilled spaghetti, a child with a fever, and a rift with a friend with a new perspective when I tell Him who He is, when I tell my heart who He is.

So I look up.

I take a passage of Scripture that speaks a truth about God and I repeat those words back to Him. I let my mind clear a space in my heart to receive. He writes back and reminds me of the times when I've seen this very truth activated in my life. I praise Him more for that reminder. I wait; I listen. Pray back. Speak back. Sing back. Write back.

When I look up, I see up.

I fix my eyes on who He is instead of what I'm not. As I blow-dry my hair or drive to the gym or step on another Lego, my thoughts linger on His beauty, not on my lack.

I'm learning to behold something other than myself.

Because you become what you behold.

I still trip over toys that creep out of their keeping places and my eye fixes on the pile of crumbs in the corner that my broom missed last night. My glass count is still slowly diminishing as slippery little hands learn to unload the dishwasher. I sometimes walk by the mirror and glimpse greasy fingerprints on my shirt, lunch's leftovers on me. I still crave quiet mornings alone even as I welcome chatter and footsteps from our full bedrooms.

The muss still speaks loudly in our home.

But God is showing me that His aroma can rise up out of and even over the chaos. His Word is seeping into my heart as I scrub dishes. Thoughts of His nature quicken my pulse when I am still in sweatpants, while the children chat over breakfast cleanup or lunch preparation. Adoration is working its way into my thought life, here.

Monotony is showing itself as a new opportunity to converse

and commune and beat back old, stale thoughts. His Word and His whisper are becoming central to tying shoes for the hundredth time.

Jesus is big in my small, unseen moments.

Glorious monotony.

He came for these very days.

I discovered a new mark on the wall, minutes after remembering that the cabinet door was severed from its hinges by the weight of a child who had used it as a stepping stool. Another thing I had not yet added to my honey-do list.

My mind dove from a visionary focus to the limping cabinet and the new wall mark, not to mention the tiny scraps of paper embedded in the carpet threads from yesterday's craft project.

I instantly flashed back to the pristine home we'd kept for nearly eight years before it was infiltrated by rubber duckies and dolls and fingerprints. What would the me who lived in that house think of this life now?

My mind roiled.

Nate and I once climbed into bed each night with lights dimmed by choice and not to hide the dust. We lived quietly.

I love quiet.

Motherhood breeds a new kind of weakness.

Their hearts beat and bleed and flutter, and all of those movements are in my palm to shape. Most days I'm grossly underqualified.

Who, even, is capable of this responsibility?

I had all these thoughts before breakfast. But it turns out the cabinet was the least of my concerns.

As I gathered everyone for the day, she burst. She looked at me with cavernous eyes, her mouth spewing words that had been buried deep within years that most children never had to know. All of her questions of God and of the years of orphanhood He'd allowed for her were funneled into one emotion—anger—and at one target—me.

She wasn't drunk on rage; she was broken.

My child, who lived most of her days with us lightfooted and delightful, had stumbled across a release valve, and I was there to absorb the release.

She spoke venom, and I listened. She fought and pushed, hoping I would leave like everyone else, and I held her.

I had no answer, so I hugged instead of spoke, pushing back her hair with my fingers while I whispered prayers over this dark surge that startled both of us.

We had no resolution that day. Not with her heart, not with the cabinet door.

Some might call it a wasted day. The young wife who, years ago, kept the house spotless and her life quiet might wonder, *What happened?*

If the cabinet door and the mark on the wall and all the little bits of paper weren't enough to remind me that I couldn't keep up with this new calling, the vacancy in my daughter's eyes that day convinced me. I stood at the end of me, in the mess of me, flat broke while trying to embrace the richness that being Mommy is supposed to bring.

Motherhood forges its own hunger.

And my hunger is revealing this: motherhood's greatest fulfillment is not when children become vibrant God-followers who change the world for Him. Though this goal is certainly high on my list, I would be left bereft in the day-to-day reality of parenting if my eyes were on this alone. If this is my *highest* goal, then what am I to do when anger floods her limbs and his heart seems stuck, when I'm waiting and praying but not yet seeing fruit? If my chief end as a mother is anything less than knowing Him and carrying His glory in my life, I will walk through these years empty.

I have an opportunity that neither the mundanity of motherhood nor my children's not-yets will ever thwart. I can find Him, right here. And in searching Him out, I can invite His technicolor majesty in and through what might otherwise be grays.

I learned this when life bore, heavily, down on me. I was learning it again through the hunger and the feast of my motherhood.

I can grow in intimacy with Him, anywhere.

When I hear God speak over the beautiful crucible of parenting's repetition and its unknowns, when I invite Him into both of those aches, I have an opportunity to adore Him through the story my household is living.

Some days that story feels tedious. Other days, like the many when I push her hair back and whisper prayers over her unfinished edges, are laced with beautiful opportunity. Could it be that both offer the same invitation?

I could spend most days looking for the golden moment ahead, when the gold is already in front of me.

Available for every messy minute.

For Your Continued Pursuit

2 Corinthians 4:17 | 1 Peter 5:10 | Jeremiah 17:9 | John 17:3 | Proverbs 24:16 | Lamentations 3:23 | Psalm 121:1 | Isaiah 43:4 | Psalm 27:4 | 2 Corinthians 3:18 | Psalm 5:3 | Matthew 10:29 | Matthew 22:37–38

thirteen

I SEE YOU

"I have called you friends."

As life wove itself around the undergirding story of my barrenness, I couldn't always tell what might send me right back to the dull ache or sharp pain of my lack, though baby showers seemed consistently to take me to that place.

Why do I do this to myself? I wondered again, smiling for the camera, sitting next to the guest of honor as she opened gifts.

She spoke, candidly, among friends—sisters, some with wombs opened and many who hadn't yet borne children—of the moment of her first baby's birth when weeping ensued and her body released new life. They leaned in, some curious, others knowing.

I distanced myself as I listened, knowing that if I engaged with what she was saying I might just break, right there on the couch beside her. I hid, inside, working my face so that it didn't reveal the bleeding I felt internally. She knew something so glorious that my years of asking still hadn't given me, and at this stage, it wasn't the cuddles and baby-fresh skin and monumental "firsts" that allured me. It was the experience of having a body that did what it was supposed to do.

Hers was apparently majestic—holy, other—and mine damaged.

❧

Morning hadn't yet broken, but I had.

This friend's story, shared the night before, had wearied me. Again. Not just the story, but that she didn't seem aware of how much her words might pierce my heart. The shower was about her, not me, but I felt so deeply unknown in my pain amid her descriptions of childbirth.

Loneliness beckoned me that black-sky morning. It was a familiar place to go. But this time, I had new words to remember.

Last night, in the midst of her story and the murmurs of others and the pull of my mind beyond that room, He whispered to me: *I see you.*

In a world of voices and faces and experiences where I don't fit in, in a version of motherhood that forgot me, Someone sees me.

He knows me.

On other mornings, I often slid into a line of thinking that wrapped itself around me like a noose. I'd made a habit out of going there, like pressing on a bruise to gauge its pain. But that day His pull was stronger. His words were louder than those of my child-rich friend. More, His words would use hers not to crush me but to transform me.

I opened my Bible to an account I'd read more than a hundred times:

She saw Him in a crowd and stretched out a desperate reach. She didn't see herself worthy of a chosen moment, but she dove for an accidental healing. *Forget touching Him; I'll take just a brush with His clothes.*

She bore up under the weight of being unhealed. Jesus was her lottery, her only chance.

The crowd that often lost her, that overlooked her, that misunderstood the person underneath, was not one she could blend in with this day.

The Father, the Son, and the Spirit knew her.

He saw her.

A life of blood spilled out and the God-man who was not far from spilling His own blood told her to have good cheer. She was once broken and neglected, but this day she was noticed.

He saw her.

He looked beyond the years of shame she wore as a veil—she didn't know herself without it—and into her heart.

She lived reproach, but He saw faith. He declared over her what *He* saw in her, which was, of course, who she truly was. She walked away from that moment new, not just because her body was healed but because He spoke, deep calling to deep.

I know her road.

Her hour is my hour.

I am hunched, ashamed, buried in the crowd, but reaching out a desperate hand toward Him.

Over and over I learn that I don't need a physical healing to receive a heart healing.

I see you.

He spoke to me that morning of the strength in my heart though my body failed me. He reminded me of the underground healing that the past decade had witnessed, though it had not yet surfaced in the form of a burgeoning belly. He whispered truth that began to mend parts of me I didn't know were broken.

He is not thrown, as I am, by my loneliness. He isn't sidelined here. His heart leans in where mine retreats, because these moments aren't stolen. They are purposed for a different kind of receiving.

I don't need to duck. I need to reach. To be desperate.

The night I felt, again, cursed among the blessed was the night I caught His eye. The night I knew His comfort, His power, more deeply.

In that place of rest, head against His chest, is where I realized that knowing that God sees *me* frees me actually to see *Him*. Feeling misunderstood turned into the revelation that I am fully understood. All along, I had been. My discomfort with not fitting in, with missing out on my gender's best, becomes the moment when I am crowned.

I see you, He said. I was both exposed and safe because I was fully loved, relished.

And now I want to show you more of Me.

How could I recount everyday moments with my children to friends and family who asked, "So how are things going?"

Every day held a new chance for conflict. The children with each another—strangers learning to be siblings overnight and encouraged, by us, to be friends. The children with us. And then, the deepest layer: the children against the God-man who had received them orphaned but spoke over them "adopted."

Their lives were a forced immersion in a foreign world. They didn't even know how to dream about having a family like this. There were bound to be disruptions.

But the disruptions we'd grown accustomed to felt inexplicable to others. Having four former orphans, all of them recently agitated by a crazily unnatural transition, it was easier not to explain than to try to make sense of what was in no way normal, even to us who walked in it every day.

As a mother, I hesitated to join in light conversations about sibling rivalry or potty training. *Will I always feel lonely, distant from other mothers?* I wondered.

A whisper emerged from this season that I began to recognize as the anthem of the perverse underground railroad of motherhood, and of life in general: *No one can understand.*

It was the same old toxin in a new season. Four kids in two years, arriving with, collectively, more than fifteen years of fatherlessness. Adoption had made family addition more like multiplication for us. I was a step away from training bras with my girls, but it felt like I'd only just met their infant hearts. We were full, seams busting with life and pain and tears and beauty.

I created a different litany, a case before God, of why this "hard" was different, why this season was unbearable and these nuances of adoptive-mama life could not be understood by another. *It's not like their hard, or the hard I had before*, I grumbled.

Until His breath broke the sheen around my newly hardened heart. Until that tiny phrase came back to me: *I see you.*

This was not about them—the children, the mess, the chaos, the shards of their lives I was left holding; this was about me.

This was about Him.

Any piece of me the world couldn't understand was another piece left for His retrieval. Any severed circumstance I tripped over was another chance for my Maker to make it new. And to make me new.

Hearing that same phrase, over an entirely different venue, made me feel the Father's understanding eye boring deeper into my soul.

He saw me. He knew me. He knew my "now" moments— unexpected meltdowns, my day gone awry, this life bursting, and my feeling I could barely manage.

He didn't stand distant, but He spoke in: *I see you.*

The moments when complications in my girlfriends' lives kept them from standing close enough to witness my weakness against my children's weakness and to see my knees buckled, not bent—they were His moments. The times when it took too long to explain the fissures in my children's hearts, and their actions, which were so beyond typical for their age—they were His to hear. To see.

He hid me. For Himself.

Holy loneliness. Purposed loneliness.

When I felt torn between helping children find lost socks and their own identities, He said, *Here is where you'll find Me, watching each of your minutes.*

The moments that the world doesn't witness are always His to see.

The fifty or so people who gathered for this small weekend conference felt safe to me, though I didn't know all of them. The environment itself was safe. I wasn't there with my story. I got to be anonymous, this night, to the strangers in the room and the friends who'd made it like home.

Not long after worship ended came the request. Such a simple, biblical concept—"we're praying for those who are sick in their bodies"—can carry weight for someone with a limp like mine.

Many raised their hands by lifting their bodies—brokenness abounds in this world. The man without hearing in one ear and the woman with a neck injury. *Have the others had their crutches for years or days?* I wondered.

Immediately I felt isolated, but it was an isolation of my own making.

I was a month out from completing yet another year of not-yet-fertility. It wasn't at the top of my mind in my very full life — until it had to be.

As humble ones received prayer, I got lost in my thoughts.

What was it about this simple plea and these faith-filled people who left me feeling bereft every time their requests for prayer were made? Why did another's potential healing leave me lonely?

They cried out, and I cried.

I really couldn't hide my story. I wore it wherever I went.

It had escalated over the prior week. Little vignettes, one after another, in which I felt less heard, less understood.

I had tried to use words to describe pain that was word-less and sought to make my story palatable to people who hadn't lived it. I looked everywhere for someone who would "get" me.

But this wasn't about their lack of understanding. It was about mine.

For years, I'd hungered for full solace in a human. It's only natural, right? We are made to connect. Brothers and sisters in Him share a bloodline that no story can trump. Or so I thought.

I had Nate. He was growing to understand my insides, just as I was also learning them. We were discovering the new front-iers within the other all the time. I also had a few dear friends who held my hand through my life's labor. They knew me.

But as I examined this craving, it was clear that I wanted more than just a huddle of bodies. I wanted a corporate understanding.

I wanted the burden of reproach to be lifted.

More than that, I wanted to wear my inner life on the outside, because the inside of me seemed to make a whole lot more sense than my physical conundrum. At baby showers and at meetings where people pray for healing and at mothers' gatherings, I wanted a sign that said, "This Casing Isn't Accurate. Please Look Inside." I wanted my circumstances, not just my heart, to show that God blessed me, that I had moved from rejected to chosen.

Never mind the gorgeous hunger that had grown over the years or the times I had seen the joy of healing bubble up and over from my children. I had my eyes on one form of external validation.

The morning before that evening conference, my feet pounded the pavement while my mind raced in step, another run morphing into a heartrending examination. I was mulling over all of these things, the week of events all pointing to one dilemma: *Why do I, in my life full of friends and love, feel lonely and disconnected?*

Unfettered words fired through my mind like a drumbeat as my feet slapped out each step. They argued, seeking to highlight the pain that came from the dissonance between my inner life in God and my seeming lack of external validation: *You are alone. No one will ever understand you.*

So that evening while the people around me prayed for healing, I stifled sobs as I considered that my broken body seemed to mask His validation of me on the inside.

Like the middle schooler whose best friend fills her head with accolades in private and disowns her in public, I lived with my wound before God. *Wouldn't this be a good time to show people what You think of me, God? It's not enough just for me to know.*

I thought back to another group of bodies assembled in a room for prayer — the night my fifteen-year-old heart gave over to the life-and-death journey of belief. Since then, my inner life had become a sanctuary. Whereas I once couldn't sit still for minutes without leaping up again to make an "impact for God," I'd now tethered myself to my time with Him.

Morning, noon, and night called forth praise from me, the same woman who once lived with a worst-case-scenario perspective. I sweated on my Bible over the treadmill in the winter and carried it down to my kitchen sink before breakfast. It had a home on my laundry pile and on my bathroom vanity. His Word — His person, wrapped up in the Word — was filling me. I was saying *I love You* with my life, and it was beginning to feel natural.

God spoke into my dark before the dawn each morning, and then infused my mundane mommy moments with a thrilling hunger that left me wanting more. I was taking great delight in searching Him out, knowing that a good portion of the searching meant not yet finding.

We were new in love, He and I — just years into this, except His love was age-old and mine was only recently awakened.

But when I stepped across the threshold of my closed-blind prayers and into the world, I took on a new way of measuring.

No longer were these inner exchanges sufficient. I wanted more than sweet times of prayer. I wanted *justice*.

I believed that only outward validation would show that I was blessed, not cursed. I wanted proof that the One who poured over me in private would endorse me in public. Proof could come in only one way, I thought.

My body must bear the blessing.

But it didn't.

What He told me in secret wasn't yet intended to have its consummation in public.

He offered something better. My bitter waiting and pain were sweet to Him. They had christened me to exploration once. They would again and again. This was the deepest blessing I could wear.

For me to stay alive on the inside—to stay unoffended by God—I didn't need to know the outcome, nor did I need for anyone to know what He was doing in me. I needed to know Him, the God who is limitless and available for my exploration.

Months had turned to years of exploration—years of communion—and in my novice and narrow understanding of God, I had assumed this communion was mature. But communion is blessedly more than a moment's rush. It's a lifestyle of ever pressing in and up. Communion means forever molting, always shedding old and gaining new.

Though I'd touched something—Someone—that was stirring me crazy with a love no circumstance could quench, I had only just begun. Though I'd felt the hem of His cloak, He would bring Himself near enough for me to smell His skin.

For Your Continued Pursuit

Matthew 6:4 | Psalm 40:5 | Luke 8:43–48 | Psalm 34:18 | Galatians 4:6 | Isaiah 41:21 | Revelation 21:5 | Psalm 91:4 | James 5:14–16 | Colossians 2:2 | Psalm 63:1 | Jeremiah 29:13 | John 7:34 | 1 Corinthians 4:5 | Psalm 19:9–11 *fourteen*

THE ONE WHO REMEMBERS

"God ... who calls those things which do not exist
as though they did."

We were all packed in, beginning our cross-country trip back home, the home the children had now known for months. Out of the blue, the one most emotionally steady among them burst through the comfortable silence created as six sets of eyes fixed on the landscape outside of the windows.

"Why did she leave me?" she sobbed.

I tried to absorb the shock. This was a first for her. What had triggered this?

"Why did my birth mommy leave me?" she bellowed. And then she began to wail.

While my mind was running through potential responses, the one behind her joined in, wet-cheeked already himself (whether from sympathy or empathy, I wasn't sure).

I was still floundering to respond while the third, beside her, chimed in, "Why did my birth mommy have to die? Why didn't I ever get to know her?"

By that time I was crying too, just as I am now, as I type. How could one car, one family, hold all this pain?

Finally, the fourth found her voice, through whimpers. "Why is God letting my birth mommy die?"

I was stunned.

Though our goal was to raise wholehearted children, I didn't expect we'd need to discuss their severed places this soon—with all of them.

Who are we to walk them over this glass?

If my impression of Him came through the lens of me, I would fold underneath this calling. We would never get from here to wholeness. Walking with Him, for their sakes, meant walking with a firmer grasp on the Unseen—a tighter grip on His Word and who He is. Partnering with Him, for their sakes, meant walking in a hope of what we'd not yet seen during their lives.

God put four in our back seat to whom He would show Himself good, even in all their pain.

I would relearn this as I relived it.

Like Adam, I would get to partner with my Maker as He remade my children's hearts.

The scene was familiar. As our house became a child's home, all that was buried in those four young hearts rose above ground.

When I came upstairs, Nate had been holding her for nearly an hour, my child birthed on another continent. She scratched his arms and resisted his hold, full of shame and fighting the very thing her body most craved. She wanted to reject him before he could reject her. She was her mother's daughter.

These are the days Nate and I are learning to celebrate, not avoid. These are the days we have the opportunity to tell her, again, in her weakest moments, that we will never leave. These are the days when we verbalize His unnatural love.

"I love you," Nate whispered, again and again. Quiet truth against loud lies.

His hands stroked her hair away from her long forehead as if they'd known that smooth skin when it was baby fresh. Love works every angle to make itself familiar.

"No matter what you do, I will always love you," he said, his strong arms unrelenting against her writhing, familiar with what the strength of this hold could do for a weak heart.

No one wiped your tears, little girl, when they were innocent. And here they are now, aged but not mature. Though it appeared that only Africa's dust received your pain, wet and crude, there was Another, bottling each drop.

Someone saw you.

We started praying into her the opposite of what we perceived from her behavior. We weren't looking to oppose what we saw, but as we asked God to help us understand her heart, we realized that much of the whirlwind around her was born from many long days patterned in the same direction. She had made a habit of living in anarchy, fending for herself. Now here she was with a dormant beauty that had never been given permission to flourish under all those years of street life.

I was tired of too many years taking gulps of worst-case scenario expectations. This time, I tried God's perspective first. We prayed it, said it, spoke it over her and to her. We spoke it to ourselves too. He was bringing forth beauty, refinement, and gentleness.

All the things one might say she wasn't were who, we believed, He was saying she is.

One morning, her sister crawled into my lap and confessed yet another grievance. This sibling we'd been praying for with such intention was "hurting her heart."

It was not a surprise; I'd witnessed some of what she referred to. One learns to bully while living on the slum streets, as she did her first four years of life. She survived by putting others underneath her finger.

We talked it out. God was clearly using this to develop compassion for the broken in my child's heart. As we wrapped up our conversation, I said, "Let's pray and ask God how He sees your sister. Let's ask Him to give us His eyes for her."

We prayed, waited, listened.

My daughter broke the silence: "Elegant. The word elegant just came into my mind, Mommy."

Though perhaps found in a book we'd read months ago, *elegant* was certainly not part of our everyday vocabulary. God spoke through the mouth of a six-year-old babe to confirm the course we'd charted in prayer. He was making my child new and even telling her siblings about it.

God initiates beauty, and it was that beauty that He saw when He looked through the skin of her past into her heart.

He had another word to speak over her life. A better word. His love wasn't seeking to label what she wasn't; His love was calling forth who He had made her to be, through the mouth of her sister.

His love for her was unnatural, and we would join Him in loving her unnaturally.

I don't know her first word. I don't know when she rolled over or started to crawl. I didn't see her crack her first smile.

Those hours that babies study the creases on their mothers' faces aren't wasted; they are foundational.

She feels it too. I watch her brood over new mothers and

their babies as her eyes become darkened corridors into years she's never had with me. Her understanding of her pain can, some days, be like a long, lonely hallway.

So we adore, as a family. When healing is working its way in but isn't yet ready to be a conversation, we adore the Healer. Their hearts need to learn to look up just as much as mine does.

On one night, as they wrapped their jammie-clad selves around each other and us for our adoration, we adored Him as the God who remembers. We were on the letter *R* as we worked our way through the alphabet. Each letter, assigned to a different attribute of God and an accompanying verse, had become our little family guide for adoration.

That night I saw again that to children whose pasts seemed unwitnessed (because isn't so much of parenting making yourself a witness in those day-to-day moments?), having a God who remembers unlocks something inside of them.

His four-year-old words reminded me: "Thank You, God, for remembering me when my Ethiopian mommy wasn't around."

He had words for concepts too big for his young mind to fully conceive.

Then my girl followed.

"Thank You for remembering when I got my ears pierced, even though I don't remember."

I caught Nate's eyes and he gave me the look that said, *We just stumbled onto something holy.* Her words, too, were too big for her.

An initiation that most girls anticipate for years and then treasure in memory was lost to her. Another unwitnessed mile marker.

But wait, there was a Witness.

He was big enough to send us across the ocean to get this child on the day she'd asked Him to have us come, and He was big enough to remember the day she got her ears pierced.

He is the God who remembers.

To her, He is the God who remembers not because He remembers her birth or her adoption or the skills He has given her to use for His kingdom one day. To her, He is the God who remembers because He remembers when she got her ears pierced.

He remembers the first word we didn't hear. He remembers when she emerged from her biological mother's body and when her moist eyes first opened to the world outside the womb. He remembers her infant toes. He remembers when she rolled over for the first time, and when she took her first step. He heard her baby babble. He knows, intimately, every small moment of her grand life.

We learn to search by learning the One who searches us, the One who remembers.

Every adoptive parent longs for secure attachment with their child, but its absence can be easy to miss. We did.

He was plump and happy. We assumed he was finding security in our home and schedule.

As we walked into our first mommy-and-me children's music class, I relished feeling tiny hands clasped around my fingers for safety.

I wanted to be their safety.

But like many firsts before and after, the day was more layered emotionally than I thought it would be.

We passed an acquaintance on the way in, one who knew

our story but hadn't yet met the children. Caleb moved from a polite hello to a warm embrace. It was odd enough for me to notice. *He must really sense a receptivity in her,* I thought. *Or maybe she's just good with children.*

The music started in the room crowded with mommies and children and strollers and carriers and sippy cups. Then during one of the songs, the children were allowed to run to the stage, grab an item to dance with, and "return to your mommies." I held my arms open to Caleb after he retrieved his item, waiting for him to find himself back at home in my lap. Then I watched as my son bolted toward a friend sitting beside me and affectionately clasped his arms around her neck.

Something isn't right, I thought.

The chorus repeated, the children ran forward again, and Caleb retraced his steps.

Nate and I had read books about this phenomenon — attachment, or the lack thereof; we just hadn't witnessed it yet. Envy took over any inkling toward understanding in my mind that day. *He wants her more than me.* My brain got put on hold while my heart boiled.

His generous trust in others, beyond us, continued.

I supposed that seasoned moms weren't as susceptible to all the emotions that can come from a child who responds to his mail carrier the same way he responds to his mother, but I wasn't that mature. It hurt to watch my little guy find safety in people not yet classified "safe." Wet kisses on strangers' faces, no matter how enamored those strangers were with him, made me feel sick.

So Nate and I hunkered down.

We guarded Mommy-Caleb time fiercely. I attached him to me through all of my daily tasks. I spoon-fed him, this one who could feed himself. I scooped food and brought the spoon close to my eyes in an effort to bring his eyes to mine before tenderly making a game out of something you normally do only with babies. We brushed skin-against-skin at night with his face tucked into my neck. I wanted him to learn my scent, for it to be as familiar to him as his own.

I fed my boy a bottle (this one who was too old for it) and gave him nighttime lullabies from tight within my grasp.

We prayed for God to attach his heart to mine.

For me to love a child who couldn't—who wouldn't—love me discriminatingly required me to believe God's unseen love for him. To love him in the uncertainty of when that love might be reciprocated required me to choose hope over fear. If I lived the fear that this child might never love me back—that he'd forever be an orphan, dressed as a son—my movements toward him would mean nothing.

He was learning love, and so was I.

Months after this intense hedging-in during our typical bedtime routine, he spread a grin wide across his face and said, "I get to cuddle with Mommy." Our bedtime habits had moved from routine to desire.

Minutes later, he said almost in a whisper, as if he wasn't convinced he should make this request, "Don't leave, Mommy."

He had a tie to me. And my tie to him was hope imparted.

I found her holed up in her closet. She'd scooted the stool from the bathroom into it to use as her chair and had folded all of her lanky legs and arms between the clothes and shoes.

She was hunched over her Bible.

When I asked her what she was doing, she said, "Mommy, I

just want to be with Jesus." This, after her previous night's bed-time prayer: "I want to know You more than I know You now."

She hadn't lost that deep connection to God we saw in our early days with her.

I once feared that the only love she could muster would be directed upward, toward Him, the One who had been her protector. Now, even as she drew closer to Him, I could see her softening to human embraces.

She was coming alive.

She shed tears over her sin, sewed clothes for the baby doll that wasn't hers, hugged the sister she hurt with unkind words, and trumpeted her little brother's successes over her own.

"Mommy, you hurt my feelings," she confessed after I had inadvertently said something embarrassing to her.

She could feel. Hollow eyes were beginning to fill with light.

God wasn't done with her when He brought her into our home. He'd only just begun to restore.

My weak voice, coming from my weak understanding, was part of His work in piecing her back together. Even now, in the daily activities and relationships of our family, He made me her prophetic voice. Even now, when my words trembled and the understanding behind them was like fresh paint. I spoke what I didn't yet know and tasted change in me as I saw my words take shape in her.

God was grabbing my hand, across her story, and calling me up and out of where I had been and into who He was mak-ing me to be, just as I was doing for her.

"I think my heart is growing, Mommy." She said it quietly against the hum of the washer and the spray of the kitchen faucet on soiled dishes. She didn't pause for my reaction. She was thinking out loud as she clumsily worked a broom twice her size underneath the lip of the kitchen cabinets.

"How so, sweetheart?" I asked when her words sank in.

"What?" She was startled that I had entered her realization, which to her wasn't that significant. "Well, I thought in my head, 'Oh, I don't want to sweep tonight,' but I didn't say it out loud; I just started sweeping," she recounted. "And I think my heart grew?" Her declaration was now a question.

"Oh, baby girl, it did!" I declared it for her as I scooped up that girl who was too big to be held but was starved for a mama's clasp.

This was the child who, not too long before, went low when the sun went down, night after night. The one who unraveled at my feet every evening as we did our nightly routine. The one with the melting countenance over which I prayed daily as I looked for snail-like signs of improvement.

We rarely shared stories with others of this emerging one because we knew that while we, as her parents, had grace and hope for her story, others often reacted with pity. They didn't know what to do with her inconsistent behavior.

But she was finding a new identity. She was walking out the fulfillment of our feeble prayers.

Her heart was growing. Pain had made space.

I still had on my sweat-stained workout clothes and sneakers when her interruption became that day's agenda. We laid, nose-to-nose, on my bed and I stared into eyes that weren't hazel like mine and I saw myself in them. She fumbled to find the right words to ask: *Why? Why all this pain?*

She'd inherited her mama's question.

She began to tell me stories. Nate and I had held space for those words, for whenever they would come. But now, pouring from her lips, they sounded like echoes in a cave. In a tomb. Their noise reverberated within me—sadness, grief, anger. Her American counterparts had been learning to ride bikes in the summer while she had lived dirty under the sun's burn. Glimpses into her everyday life, so recent, felt like horror to my Western existence.

Moments before, I had walked through the quiet haze that rested on my neighborhood and asked God for her heart. Even so, I felt unprepared to know how to respond as she plopped that heart into my lap.

I prayed while she spoke: *Help*. How do you teach a child—who has lost more in a lifetime than I can understand—a whole new way of seeing life and God?

This is what I said: "Since the beginning of time, He intended you for me, and me for you."

She asked me, skeptically, "How do you know?"

Sprawled on my bed—same comforter but different home—I told her about the vision I'd had all those years ago of her crawling on my bed toward my arms.

"He told me about you early," I said, and my words were like balm to the questions that had become her oozing wounds. "He knew, baby girl. Even then. I saw you. He saw you. You were not forgotten."

Many spend their whole lives, even within the safety of a family, wondering whether God notices them. The pain of my little girl's story brought forth a vision—years earlier—that answered the question she hadn't yet asked.

He is near to the orphan. He is sweet against her broken-ness. He saw her. He knew her. He noticed her, then.

Every dark place has its redemption in Him. Every single one.

For Your Continued Pursuit

2 Corinthians 4:18 | Deuteronomy 31:6 | Psalm 56:8 | Romans 4:17 | Hebrews 12:24 | Psalm 136:23 | Jeremiah 17:10 | Psalm 71:5 | Psalm 139 | 1 Corinthians 4:5

fifteen

IS JESUS BEAUTIFUL?

"Abide in My love."

I woke up, lethargic. Why did the morning so often feel like it broke over me, not open for me? Before my feet touched the floor, I was remembering my friend's comment from days previous: "We're starting down this path of treatment because we don't want to have to wait *ten years* before we have a child."

She made the comment unknowingly. I had seen ten years without a baby.

She didn't want what I was living.

On my raw days, I didn't want what I was living either.

I knew well what she was resisting.

But when I scooted up next to Him, when His nearness felt as real to me as my own hands, I wanted it all. I wanted every minute of those ten years and all that came before. I wanted the marriage struggles and the financial rifts. I wanted the strained friendships. I wanted the battle for my dad's life.

When I was near enough to Him to smell His skin, the rest of the world and my circumstances faded into gray. He was *that good*.

I'm not typically an optimist. I never have been. But the rub of the calluses of His hands against my story—the hands made flesh, yet encasing divinity—when no one else was looking made the painful minutes, which added up to months and then years, worth it. It wasn't worth it "one day." It was worth it already.

I was a different woman than the one I had been before my life unraveled, because God had become to me a different God than the one I'd contrived Him to be when it all was working as it should.

But what about the in-between minutes? What about the mornings, like this one, when His nearness didn't feel near and I was stuck on one comment from a friend and I couldn't get my eyes off me? Could the mere memory of the last time that He lifted me out of myself be enough to carry me in the moments when all I could feel was the reproach of what I didn't have?

That morning I moved from my bedside to my chair for prayer, and then, an hour later, got ready for a morning run. All the while my thoughts traveled from her comment and what it revealed—*No one else wants my story; most people live their lives avoiding it*—through self-pity and back to that place of feeling stuck. Lacking. Cursed.

I'd had a dream, years before, in which I left something I wanted in my eighth-floor hotel room. When I went to retrieve it, I realized that there was no way to get back to that floor. Up the stairs and down again, I discovered doors to every floor but mine. The elevator had a button for the eighth floor, but even though I furiously pressed it and it lit up, the elevator never once stopped there.

On mornings like that one, that dream came back to me. *Am I stuck forever? Will what I want most always taunt me?* On mornings like that one, I learned a one-word prayer: *Help*. It was all I could mutter before Him.

I closed the front door behind me for my run, feeling sluggish but, even more, not wanting to return to the staleness I'd felt in my prayer room.

Out the door and up the street, getting lost in the prison that my mind had become as I ran, *help* was my exhalation. The only thing I had with me, other than worship music (which seemed to fail me when these toxic musings were louder than the words in my earbuds), was the verse I'd scribbled reluctantly in my Moleskine journal just before I'd left: "As the Father loved Me, I also have loved you; abide in My love."

Help was my doorway from dregs of bitterness to the place of vulnerability. Then His Word framed what my mind couldn't.

I crested the first hill of the run I'd done hundreds of times, muscle memory moving my feet without my thinking, and I moved out of the muscle memory of bitterness that often didn't require much thinking either. I didn't *feel* loved that morning as I saw her face in my mind when she made that remark, herself not wanting the position of reproach that I was living.

But His Word had something else to say.

Minutes like those were perhaps even more critical for my heart than the ones spent in my prayer room when I felt His arms around me, encompassing my pain.

Oh, how I had grown to love the nearness I felt from Him when I left a room full of people, unnoticed but knowing He had been waiting to commune with me the whole time.

But what about His nearness when I didn't feel Him?

That verse — the phrase I repeated as my feet created a cadence on the pavement beneath me — was about seeing Him as near, even when I didn't feel Him.

I had left the house, flat. Empty. Grumpy. But as I began to repeat the truth I didn't feel, with which I didn't even want to engage, on a morning when I couldn't sense Him close to me, I awakened to love.

I let adoration fill the gap between when God wildly meets my hunger and when hunger just feels like an empty cry for help.

I lingered on the verse and what it means, in adoration.

He loves me like He loves His Son. He invites me into a holy, other, familial kind of love. Every portion of my story hides within it His intentions. Even my story itself can abide.

I couldn't see God's eyes as I moved from thinking about all my lack to who He is, but I could hear His Words. Both my moments in His arms and the moments when I could only breathe *help* would repattern my thinking.

I hit the returning point on my run and circled back home, noticing, instead of the pavement and the grooves in the road where the tar had gathered and the weeds crept up through the cracks, the red-tailed hawk perched on the telephone wire and the sun burning through the clouds and the backs of the tree leaves that were shades lighter when the wind exposed them.

The trail of thinking that followed my friend's comment was really just masking hunger. I couldn't respond to that hunger, or keep growing into who He was calling forth from me, without looking up.

God wanted my heart-cracked-open cries and He wanted my everyday minutes.

Abide in My love. When you feel orphaned. When the words and silences of others hurt you. When you are alone. Stay here. Live here. You are loved, understood. Sara, you are seen in this home.

I was doing dishes in the kitchen when I heard the chorus of a song on an old playlist faintly playing on our iPod in the background.

I sang the lyrics to myself while rinsing food off plates, distracted by the task and unaware of the words, until I remembered. These words describing the worship that comes from the place of suffering had rocked me to sleep at night when my night was starless. These words were my lullaby when I was without words for my pain.

This wasn't just background music to me once. It was my anthem.

I had listened to that song while curling my body into a ball in my bed and on my bedroom floor and on the family room couch, reaching for words that I didn't feel in an effort to frame my story with His truth. I had listened to that song in my car while driving home from baby showers, singing its truths over myself and trying to believe them. I had listened to that song in my bedroom after arguments with Nate, in my loneliness on Sunday afternoons, and in my prayer room as I brought my pain, again, to a Father who never tired of my open heart.

I stood in my kitchen and wept over the years past. My pain had not disappeared, but it had diminished. Circumstances were no longer at the peak of perplexity. But the music took me back to the waves of grief and loss and all the questions wrapped around a season I wasn't sure would ever end.

Just as soon as I remembered the sharp moments of pain, I remembered the nearness of the Father, who came right into the middle of them. Both memories—the sting of pain and the balm of His coming to me in my pain—were vibrant, real again, but it was now as if His presence during that pain overshadowed the memory of the pain itself.

There in my kitchen, though, over dishes, I realized that memories of my closeness to Him in that pain were not enough to sustain me. Nostalgia wouldn't carry me with strength into the next season, much less the next day.

I had been a fifteen-year-old girl riding the bus back from Camp Storer, tracing her finger in the fog that formed on the windows and thinking about the decision she'd made the night before. That moment was life changing. But that moment and its memory weren't enough to sustain me.

I had been a teenager rocking under the summer sky on my backyard swing, praying sweet prayers of trust and faith. But those evenings weren't enough to sustain me.

Even the times I'd found Him during my sharpest pain weren't enough to hold me up under later griefs.

Intense seasons of spiritual growth provoked me, fed me even as they increased my hunger, but once they became memories, they could no longer be my sustenance.

The lowest points of pain and some of the sweetest touches of Him came back to me as I heard the words of that song that had broken my fall and cradled me. I knew my life would need hundreds, thousands of such moments across my life for my heart to grow. I couldn't eat yesterday's bread today. I had to continue to hunger both in the pain and in the ordinary.

My very worst days were purposed. My current days, the ones that stung but didn't leave me folded on the floor, were also purposed. It would be naive to think that future years wouldn't hold more pain. It would be just as naive to think that finding Him in the pain would be my only story.

But in all seasons—times of searing grief, times of great redemption, times of the mundane—every single moment was pregnant with His whisper: *Come, let us run together. Come find Me. Here.*

❧

"A satisfied soul loathes the honeycomb, but to a hungry soul every bitter thing is sweet." I don't want to be a hungry soul just for a season. I want to live hunger. This is what draws me to Him. This is what fills every single bitter circumstance with the opportunity to know Him more. This is what brings me to the sweetness of His presence.

And hope happens here at this nexus of bitter and sweet.

I will not talk myself out of hope, hiding behind Scripture to support all my reasons for being "wise" and "measured" in my responses to the not-yets in my life.

Because when I choose hope, when I choose to engage in that awkward intimacy of believing that He might say no while asking expectantly that He say yes, He gets the most beautiful part of me.

Hope is my precious oil, mingling with tears to wash His feet.

Hope, and the vulnerability it brings, is what moves His heart.

Hope, and how it draws me to Him, means that not one of those minutes curled up in pain was lost, not one of those minutes of closeness with Him is forgotten, not one of those negative pregnancy tests was wasted.

I choose to stand with those at the edge of flames and say with my life, "Our God whom we serve is able to deliver us from the burning fiery furnace, and He will deliver us from your hand, O king." And I choose to say too, "But if not . . ." Hope is still worth it when my desire becomes one crazy, beautiful offering to Him.

Though pain rages on this side of eternity, I can find His

words, His music, His arms. I can discover that our greatest testimony isn't found in those moments of victory over weakness or even in the moments of hope fulfilled.

It is found in waiting, wanting, adoring. It is found in hunger.

I had just wrapped myself around her little frame, settling her in for her afternoon rest, when she pulled her head back and asked, almost wistfully, "Mommy, is Jesus beautiful?"

She didn't know what day it was for me when she asked. She didn't know her question needed to be my question too. And I didn't realize that her question might be the umbilical chord that bound us, one to the other.

It was my dad's birthday, a day harder for me than even the anniversary of his death. The day of his death was only recently on my calendar, but for my whole life, December 16 had meant something. When I was a child, December 16 meant that we gathered. Well, we always gathered; dinnertimes together were an everyday tradition. But on birthdays, we *gathered*, cake and the honored guest's favorite meal to boot.

I remember the year I had money from a first job and used it to give him a colored-patch sweater (when sweaters like that were still in style). I remember the years before that, when Santa's Secret Shop took over our school library early enough that I could find my dad a birthday gift among the rest of the tchotchke sold to starry-eyed children for pennies.

The picture I framed of the Swiss Alps, the one I took when I was hiking their base on a college exploration trip, is one I now own. I gave it to my dad on his birthday the year after I traveled Europe. He'd stayed up late nights during the month I was gone, his enthusiasm for what I must be doing during those hours it was night in my home but daytime in Europe interrupting his sleep.

I knew all those years that gifts weren't really his thing. One year, I made him a pecan pie because our finances were so tight. He probably remembered that pie, whose ingredients cost less than ten dollars, more than he did that colored-patch sweater.

"You have a zest for life, Sara," my dad used to tell me. I had no idea, when my eyes were that wide with zest, what I might need to walk through to really know zest. I had no idea what I might need to walk through to know the God-man who gave it to me. And to know in my core that He was good to me.

The morning of his birthday, I had stumbled out of bed to meet my running buddy for our weekly morning run. I didn't tell her what day it was. The grief felt easier swallowed than spoken.

The town was lit up for Christmas, but I felt the ache inside. Preoccupied and already trapped in clumsy skin, I tripped and skidded across the pavement. In the dark.

Figures, I thought, nursing my pain instead of seeing it as the avenue I knew it to be. *Figures on a day like today, I'd also take a spill.* My grief wasn't just that I'd lost my dad but that so much of what I'd prayed and hoped for my broken body still felt lost. Out there, somewhere. Even physical pain triggered a reminder of that loss.

That old worst-case-scenario thinking threatened to disrupt a day that was holy. Holy because of my pain, my hunger, and my choice of how to respond.

I inhaled those stale thoughts all the way in until my daughter's voice interrupted my inner dialogue. Her question was central to how I was beginning to frame my world. She, of course, didn't know this.

Is Jesus beautiful?

With my little girl's query, God said to me, *I see you, Sara, here in your loss. Today. I see your brokenness. And I see My wholeness, tucked inside of you, being birthed.*

"Is Jesus beautiful?" I asked, repeating the question for my own benefit. "Oh, Eden. Yes. Jesus is so beautiful. Sometimes, when you look into His eyes, in your mind, you feel like you could look for hours. He's so safe and so full of life and so loving. God made Jesus' beauty to be almost overwhelming. Ask Him for yourself. Ask God to show you what Jesus looks like. I'll bet you'll see His beauty."

Oh, the grace of this child, with a past that could leave her skeptical of God's beauty, asking her mama this question in anticipation. She stared up at me with eyes that were hungry, a hunger I'd seen before in her. The answer to her question might be the very thing that carries her through her own life's pain. It might be her entry into a life of finding Him as the Healer of her once-broken, once-bitter story. It might be her gateway to hunger.

The words God gave me to respond to her question were also His words for me. A life bent toward asking that question would be my answer. And that answer would bind us, mother and daughter. Both seeking. Both hungry. Both set on finding the sweetness of Him waiting inside what the world calls bitter.

For our grief to move from pure pain to hunger required this expectant look toward Jesus' beauty. One long look strung across a lifetime of long looks.

His beauty had met my pain's hunger on the day my dad died, His arms enfolding me as only a daddy's arms can. His beauty had met my pain's hunger when the money had run out and when I slept like a stranger beside the one I'd married.

His beauty had met my pain's hunger when I logged years, not months, in the grave of barrenness.

His beauty made sense of my pain when I said yes to adoptions three and four, making the world under my roof even less understandable to those outside of it. His beauty made sense of my pain when my children's past bled across my doorstep. His beauty would make sense of the pain still to be lived on this broken earth.

Every single ache, large and small, had a response from a God who put on skin so that I might know His scent and feel His hands and live in a nearness that would forever keep me coming back to sit at His feet. This unnatural love was inching toward becoming natural for me, the one who for so many years felt she'd failed at living "well" in the natural world.

My hunger had made a path to a Man who would call me out of myself and into a story better than even the best this world could produce.

That beautiful Jesus, the One I barely yet knew.

He would make me love the hunger that drew me to Him.

"It's ruined, Mommy! I ruined it!" she said, through sobs, thrusting her Bible into my hand.

My child, who cannot yet read, mimicked her mommy by making her Bible a workbench, chicken scratches and all. Today her overzealous roulette landed her on a verse that she used a marker to "highlight." The verse was no longer visible under Crayola's ocean blue.

"Is it gone forever, Mommy?" she asked.

I assured her a sticky note with the verse handwritten on it would keep this verse from ever slipping her mind.

"Forever flagged," I said as I pulled out my pen to transcribe the verse from my Bible onto hers.

My eyes fell on a familiar passage, a life anthem. This was the verse she'd chosen:

> "Sing, O barren,
> You who have not borne!
> Break forth into singing, and cry aloud,
> You who have not labored with child!
> For more are the children of the desolate
> Than the children of the married woman," says the LORD.
> —Isaiah 54:1

My breath tightened. I'd been praying that week for the children, Nate, me—all of us—*Lord, surprise us with Yourself at our least expectant moments. Show up in our mundane. Break into our daily lives with bursts of Your glory.*

I carried her Bible downstairs to Nate's office with trembling hands. *I think this is it*, I thought. *This is what I've been praying not to overlook.*

Nate and I shared looks, not words, after he read it. A knowing had grown between us across our empty arms. We'd developed a cadence to the rise and fall of this monthly, yearly wait.

The one we'd named Hope was my message bearer on that day, an ordinary day of growing and longing and bringing both our growing and longing before Him in our pain, our joy.

Hope was our reminder that even in the waiting, it is time to sing.

For Your Continued Pursuit

John 15:9 | Song of Solomon 1:4 | Proverbs 27:7 | Luke 7:36–50 | Daniel 3:17–18 | Psalm 90:15–17 | Isaiah 54:1

EPILOGUE

What I Would Say to Her
(Written Long After the Ink Was Dry)

Nate surprised me with tulips in winter, and the card read, "To long, quiet love … and new life."

They hadn't been on my counter for twelve hours before he awoke to my sobs from the other room.

Can it be? Can it really be?

We found each other in the dark and wept a new kind of tears over this heartache that had the dust of nearly a decade.

Today we were crossing over Jordan.

Though it was February, this portion of our lives, still hanging in the balance of winter, was over.

Spring had come.

My womb had opened. I was carrying a child within.

We lingered for weeks into months cupping our hands around this sacred secret.

It even feels slightly betraying to share it here, now, but my body can no longer hide what's been warming inside.

How do you say goodbye to a season that He's used to make you into who you are?

For months I have had a conversation with her, that twenty-three-year-old bride who didn't know she was on the front end of some of the hardest years of her life.

I reach across the table from her in my mind and clasp my fingers around the parts of her story that will soon be raw and bleeding. I speak the still-nascent clarity that twelve years of walking that quiet road have produced. I want to impart to her what twelve years of finding God over all the unexpected pain will do.

I stare deep into eyes that are more vacant than she realizes and say the words of life: *Hold onto Him. This will all be worth it one day.*

I know as I say it that her life, so carefully formed around hedging herself in from all that she fears, can't possibly absorb what "worth it" might mean. After all, fear makes life small.

Her greatest vision of what constitutes being "worth it" will be, for a time, an outward expression of vindication: her body healed, her finances righted, her marriage thriving, her friendships forged. While those things are good and true and beautiful, the conversation in my mind with the twenty-three-year-old version of myself centers on something so different. Other.

Hold on, young one. He shares with you the reproach you carry. He knows that it will one day be a crown, not through new circumstances but through a new heart. In your barrenness you will know God as the Giver of good gifts. Before your body ever holds another's heartbeat inside of it, He will give you life.

I see vignettes of her life.

I watch her clench fists on her walk across the sand, alone, to that honeymoon hotel. Driven and ambitious even in her newborn marriage.

I watch her force the pedal to the floorboard as she speeds away from her parents' home, hoping she can drive and never turn back. Behind her is her father, whose brain has succumbed to a diagnosis that is becoming a verdict. And with her, still, is her barrenness.

I watch her unable to speak on the phone when she receives the news about the lost adoption paperwork. She was teetering long before that phone call. How much can bear down on one heart?

Tears burn angry down her cheeks as she reviews each loss, asking, *At what point did my life become cursed?*

I want to meet her on that road and tell her that her twenty-something life was not cursed but chosen. That the tomb is but a holding place for a body that will forever declare resurrection.

As Nate and I celebrate twelve years since the day that little boy in big-boy skin asked that naive wee thing to marry him, we tell the world outside our home that, as with Jacob's Rachel, He remembered.

Twelve years later, He remembered.

Spring.

I wanted a one-time miracle, a story I could shout from the rooftops that says, "Our God heals against all odds!" But He first gave me six long and quiet stories under this roof. Each of us preached the message of His healing with our lives, and this was only the beginning. This family of mine, we share a beautiful branding. All of us wear His scars.

Now I can only whisper the glory streaming forth with this baby announcement because it is so sacred to my story. It speaks of a healing, a remembrance, that didn't just happen the day my womb opened.

Year one of winter felt like a lifetime. Year five indicated that we'd crossed into new territory. At years seven, eight, hoping in the unseen was becoming too familiar. Yet the power of His hand as Healer was working, even then. We had hearts to be healed and understandings of Him to be mended and conversations with our Daddy to be initiated.

I lived hundreds of miracles in the winter, when the ground felt hard to the touch but life was germinating, thick, within me. My heart was revived in winter. He breathed on the fractured parts of me with a tenderness that left me lovestruck.

All the while, I couldn't let go of asking for another miracle.

If hope died, it would only be a reflection of how my perspective of Him, and what brings Him pleasure, had grown dim. To know Him is to hope for the impossible.

I thought my open womb would be the best and only glory story, but instead He let me cradle the fruit of other women's bodies. He introduced healing, our truest healing, into Nate and me in ways we never knew we needed.

My life has been living the healing that my body has only just now revealed. It will continue to do so, through the winters bound to come. A baby in my arms is not something our healing has earned, the culmination of our hope. We each have a deeper journey still.

So I lean in close to my twenty-three-year-old heart, and I whisper, *You will meet a Man in this pain who will pick up the slivers of your story and write His name on each one. Your knowing Him, alone, through this, will make every tear worth it.*

Hold onto hope. Hold onto hope. Even those closest to you will challenge it, as the world around you collapses, but hope is your greatest weapon because it is His invitation into the Unseen. Hope requires a true view of God. And that true view of God is not natural. It's from Him. One day, the Unseen will be more real to you than what your eyes can perceive.

Turning back from myself as a young bride, I wrap my arms around the girth that now holds a child. Whispering, shouting, silent, I say, *Father, I am overwhelmed by this new way You are showing Yourself to me as Healer. And I know that You are no more good today than You were a year ago. You are good ... to me.*

Winter and spring: He is Healer in both.

For Your Continued Pursuit

Joshua 3 | Romans 8:5–6 | Luke 1:37 | Job 37:5 | Genesis 30:22–23 | Romans 8:24–25 | Job 1:20–21 | Isaiah 61:11 | Isaiah 51:3 | Isaiah 64:4 | Song of Songs 2:10–13 | Romans 5:3–5

ACKNOWLEDGMENTS

The community that carved a hole in the roof and lowered me on my mat to His feet stretches across continents and all over these states. This community, which wrapped its arms around my waist and ushered me to Him for a measure of heart healing and which prayed, over years, for my body to be healed, is both cohesive and beautifully independent.

And it's for your uniquenesses in Him that I thank each one of you who formed a part.

To my agent, Curtis Yates, and his wife, Karen: you have made this process measurably more enjoyable than I imagined it to be. He has used you to debunk my fears about publishing a book and made you to be dear friends in the meantime. You so masterfully carry both attention to detail and perspective on the vision He is unfolding in a person. One of the greatest gifts of this process has been you.

To the entire Zondervan team: I am blessed to have you carry my story. Sandy Vander Zicht, I liked you from the moment I met you and was thrilled to be able, then, to work with you. Thank you for seeing this manuscript with His eyes, even in its roughest form. Brian Phipps, I'm certain you didn't miss one jot or tittle, and I got an education in writing from witnessing your craft. Elisa Stanford, He rested on you as you so skillfully handled my story and gave it wings in a way that it made me want to know *your* story even more. I have a new friend in you.

Katie Davis: is it really possible to forge a friendship with more than a dozen children and an ocean between us? Your heart for Him provokes me, and your timing in this process was beautifully indicative of how you hear Him. I love how you love. You are leading many to shed their tears over His dusty feet.

Judy Lewis, your response to His little nudge to reach out to me was paramount in this process. I feel spoiled, now, to call you my friend.

Mandie Joy Turner, you've made this little habit of adoration accessible to so many who are hungry. Your heart for Him precedes your creativity, and the rest of us benefit. (And to think Lily wouldn't be ours without you. How do you thank someone for that?)

Amy Julia Becker: one afternoon and one single email took the ceiling off my expectations of what He can do. You have spoken beautiful vision into something that I thought would forever be just a hobby.

There are ones, so dear, who are now pushing me closer to Him and ones from the days when this manuscript was barely a breath inside of me who helped teach me how to walk when I could barely crawl.

From back then:

Bill and Cindy Finley, Eric and Holly Nelson, Susan Cunningham, Chris Martin, Cathy Wicks, Trina Rogers, Mara and David Roberts, Jamie Price: you loved when we were unlovely; you lived unnatural love toward us when it wasn't easy and we weren't easy to love.

Jonathan and Julie Baker: that summer on your farm, and

your continuing faithfulness to us, has changed us. Forever. He planted a seed there, through you.

Marcy and Corban Klug: by letting us watch and pray with you, He opened our eyes to what He can do. Your friendship is rare.

To the Miami girls, who embraced me during the years when I had no idea who I was and only an inkling of who He is, especially those who've held my fragile heart these past few years (you know who you are): I love your part in my history.

And all of you continue to shape our story with your love, albeit over a distance.

And here, now:

Dana Candler and the Wednesday night group girls: each one of you so uniquely burns for Him. I haven't left one single week without being stirred to let my heart burn like yours do. *Who gets to have friends like these?* I often think.

Michelle Seidler, you and your crew had His perspective, consistently, when I wavered. I have seen His love trump fear at the hands of your encouragement.

To Russell and Eliza Joy Capps: you've traveled with us through two very different seasons and witnessed lots of our awkward growing pains in between, and you've still chosen to see us through eyes of love. Thank you.

Elizabeth Wilkerson, you put up with my immaturity at sixteen and have pushed me to dream with Him at thirty-six. Twenty years and I still feel like the adventure in Him, together, is ahead of us. Kelly Tarr, the gift of your friendship makes me worship Him. I love that I have a window into how you love Him all over the hidden pockets of your life. It's stunning. Jen Stutzman, the yes in your everyday walk redefines the beauty of adoption, and your encouragement of me embodies that.

And friends whose names aren't listed here but who held my hand at various times throughout my living this book and then my writing this book: I love the different angles of Him that each one of you reflects.

Blog readers: for so long I wanted to hit "publish" and hide underneath my chair, but He used your notes and emails and stories to ever so slowly uncoil me. There were hearts on the other side of the screen that He was touching. Thank you for so graciously handling my little art project, week after week. Thank you for being vulnerable enough to let Him speak to you through it.

Mom, Alison, and Chris—the family anchors for emotional ones like Dad and me—I have loved being all that it means to be a Welter with each of you.

To my dad: you set me up for this with all of our talks on the living room couch. Until we meet again.

Lily, Hope, Eden, Caleb, and Bo: you are five of my six favorite people on this planet. Each one of you carries such a beautiful piece of His heart for the world—and His heart for me. I am crazy about you.

Nate, the truth is *I* get to be the one. I get to see who you are when no one is looking, and your hidden life has been the greatest surprise of this marriage. Your dozens of yeses toward Him in any given day shape this family. Thank you for steadying me with your love.

To God, the famous One who made Himself famously tender to me when I least expected it: You continue to turn my understanding of You anew by Your unnatural love. Thank You for preparing for Yourself a bride and inviting me into that white when I felt stained. I love the story You write on me.

SCRIPTURE REFERENCES

one

"Blessed are those who hunger": Matthew 5:6

two

"Draw me away!": Song of Solomon 1:4

three

"Let me see your face ...": Song of Solomon 2:14

four

"For He has torn, but He will heal us": Hosea 6:1

five

"For My thoughts are not your thoughts": Isaiah 55:8

six

"You are my private garden ...": Song of Solomon 4:12 (NLT)

seven

"And I will look up": Psalm 5:3
"Your faithfulness reaches to the clouds": Psalm 36:5

eight
"Hope that is seen is not hope": Romans 8:24

nine
"He is not far from each one of us": Acts 17:27

ten
"For we were saved in this hope": Romans 8:24

eleven
"Can these bones live?": Ezekiel 37:3

twelve
"Your Father who sees in secret": Matthew 6:4
"And I will look up": Psalm 5:3

thirteen
"I have called you friends": John 15:15

fourteen
"God ... who calls those things ...": Romans 4:17

fifteen
"Abide in My love": John 15:9
"As the Father loved Me ...": John 15:9
"A satisfied soul loathes the honeycomb ...": Proverbs 27:7
"Our God whom we serve ...": Daniel 3:17
"But if not ...": Daniel 3:18

The **tenderness** of God becomes real when our precious anchors get l o o s e and we're d r i f t i n g. That terrifying moment could turn **glorious** if we stop long enough to look at His face *&* *consider Him near*.

Join us **in the daily journey** of adoration …

on Instagram, Facebook, Twitter, and the web:

@EveryBitterThingisSweet   @SaraHagerty
/EveryBitterThingisSweet   • www.EveryBitterThingisSweet.com

#EveryBitterThingisSweet